Minerva's Owl

The Bereavement Phase
of My Marriage

Minerva's Owl

The Bereavement Phase
of My Marriage

by

Carol Matthews

OOLICHAN BOOKS
FERNIE, BRITISH COLUMBIA, CANADA
2017

Library and Archives Canada Cataloguing in Publication

Matthews, Carol, 1942-, author

Minerva's owl : the bereavement phase of my marriage

/ Carol Matthews.

ISBN 978-0-88982-325-9 (softcover)

1. Matthews, Carol, 1942- --Marriage. 2. Husbands--Death.

3. Bereavement. I. Title.

BF575.G7M219 2017   155.9'37   C2017-905066-4

Cover photo by Bill Pennel.

Cover design by Vanessa Croome.

We gratefully acknowledge the financial support of the Canada Council for the Arts, the British Columbia Arts Council through the BC Ministry of Tourism, Culture, and the Arts, and the Government of Canada through the Canada Book Fund, for our publishing activities.

Published by
Oolichan Books
P.O. Box 2278
Fernie, British Columbia
Canada V0B 1M0

www.oolichan.com

Printed in Canada

For Mike, always

When philosophy paints its gray in gray,
then has a form of life grown old.
Philosophy cannot rejuvenate it,
but only understand it.
The owl of Minerva spreads its wings
only with the coming of the dusk.

G.W.F. Hegel

Contents

Bereavement is not the truncation of married love but one of its regular phases—like the honeymoon.

A Grief Observed, *C.S. Lewis*

Introduction

March, 2015. At first I wondered how that could be, but now I believe that C.S. Lewis is right. In many ways, my bereavement is not unlike the romantic days of our courtship, and the honeymoon, when we were uncertain, unfamiliar, just beginning to learn about each other. You were unknown and exotic, and when we were apart I longed for you. Later, through years of married life, you became so familiar that I could not draw a line between us. Now, since your death, you've become distinct, apart again, and my feelings of longing echo those early days. It's like falling in love again, this final phase of our marriage.

From perfect grief there need not be
Wisdom or even memory;
One thing then learned remains to me—
The woodspurge has a cup of three.

The Woodspurge, *Dante Gabriel Rosetti*

Grieving

February 25, 2012. Your death was sudden. Shocking. Just seventeen days after you were admitted to hospital. Nine days in which we thought you would recover and then eight days in palliative care. I wept for your pain, vulnerability, the indignity of it all. I wish I'd been able to do more to help you, but know that, through the years to come, I'll have to face all you endured. At length, helpless, without you.

They say our bodies are formed from stardust, and when we die we return to the stars. That sounds true. When my father died, I told my young daughter that I now thought her grandfather was up among the stars. I didn't believe in life after death, but it was easy to look up into the night sky and tell her that somehow, somewhere, he was a part of it. I would gaze at the Milky Way, the constellations of the horoscope, and think of deification. Apotheosis. The hero raised to a god-like stature.

On the day before you died, Mike, I read you a stanza of Eliot's Four Quartets, one that you'd recited to me in the first days of our courtship:

> *Garlic and sapphires in the mud*
> *Clot the bedded axle tree...*
> *The dance along the artery*
> *The circulation of the lymph*
> *Are figured in the drift of stars.*

As you lay dying, your dog asleep at the foot of your bed, our daughter Alison on one side of you and me on the other, each holding one of your hands, I assured you that it wouldn't be long until we'd all be together again in the drift of stars. I didn't know what I was saying; yet, without intention or forethought, my words were full of conviction.

Did that offer you comfort? It doesn't console me. Nothing does. The grief is more intense than I could have imagined.

Our word "grief" is derived from the Latin *graus* or *gravis*, meaning "heaviness." Grief brings a heaviness to the spirit, the psyche, the body. I sleep deeply and at length, but dread morning. I am weighed down by the loss of you.

In *A Grief Observed*, C.S. Lewis notes that the

sensation of grief is like fear. The same fluttering in the stomach, the restlessness, the yawning. For me, it is also nausea. Every morning, I awake disoriented, panic-stricken, nauseous; my whole being rejects the approach of another day without you.

The word "bereft" comes to mind, with its roots in the Old English *bereafian*—to deprive of, take away, seize, rob, despoil. Yes, you have been seized from me, ripped away. I am robbed, despoiled by my loss.

I turn to words for solace, but there are no words sufficient for this aching void. No way to describe it. And yet everyone tries. When a loved one dies, people bring the death books, and there are a great many. Even friends with whom you and I joked about the death books will find a way to bring words they think will be of comfort—a little book about loss, a distinguished author's account of bereavement, a collection of poetry, a manual on mindful grieving.

My inclination is to dismiss these books because I know in my heart that my grief is like no other, and yet I end up reading them. And I find, of course, the bereaved have much in common in their experience of loss.

I thought I was the only one who wrote letters to her dead husband until I read Natascha McElhone's *After You*. When her forty-three-year-old husband died, leaving her with two young sons and pregnant with a third, she said writing letters to him enabled her to "keep him here" long enough to come to terms with her loss. Similarly, in *The Year of Magical Thinking*, Joan Didion writes about trying to keep the dead alive "in order to keep them with us." As long as I can write to you, you are still with me, even though we are in separate worlds.

I hadn't previously read any of Daphne du Maurier's novels, but her essay "On Death and Widowhood" resonates with me. She speaks of how, to ease the pain, she wore her husband's shirts and used his pens in order to feel closer to him. I've learned that many grieving people wear their partner's shirts, sleep in their pyjamas, bury their noses in a favourite sweater to catch a hint of scent. We sit at their desks, use their pens, keep up the rituals, and try to capture threads of our partners' presence. It takes a long time to change the joint message on the telephone answering service. We don't want to let go.

In our later years, you and I sometimes talked about the predictable bereavement that one or the other of us would experience. A sort of Abbott and Costello routine like Who's on First? *Who's on first, What's on second, I Don't Know is on third.*

It would be best if I died first. I wouldn't want to leave you, but I think it would be best.

That's silly. I couldn't manage without you.

I hate to think of you on your own, but you'd manage better than I would.

I wouldn't manage at all, you idiot! I'd die without you. Whereas you would be all right. All sorts of women would come around with casseroles.

I don't want their stinking casseroles.

Maybe we should do the long swim together. Plunge into the waves and head out past the point of no return.

No, not the long swim... not yet.

Maybe we should die together in a plane crash.

Yes. On a holiday.

On the return trip, our way back from a holiday.

A predictable transition, yes, and one we often discussed, but not one we could ever plan for. As P.K. Page said in her poem "Preparation," what happens is never like what you prepared for: *It is where you are not/ that the fissure occurs/ and the light crashes in.*

In those last years I'd turn to see your face on the pillow next to mine each morning and would say, happily, "Well then, another day." You always seemed so vital, so indestructible. I was sure you would outlive me. I thought you'd live forever.

And now I envision your face out there in the starry sky in the constellation of Cancer, which is in between Gemini, the sign for you and Alison, and Leo, for our granddaughter Charlotte.

"Don't you find it strange, Nana," Charlotte asks, "that we're part of the Milky Way and yet we can see the Milky Way?"

A good question, I tell her. I feel that you are still a part of me, Mike, and yet I can only imagine you as being far away, out there in the drift of stars.

At the memorial centre I picked up your remains. You scoffed at the word "centre" being applied to buildings that were actually on the periphery of things, but that is what they always call these funeral places.

You detested false language. Well, what then about the false word for your ashes? Your remains. These are not your remains. Your remains are not only here in this little box, but everywhere around me. Later this morning I will go to Protection Island, and your remains will be on the ferry, on the roads, in our home on the waterfront. And also in the ocean where we will spread your ashes.

I remind myself that you are also in Alison and Charlotte. Your daughter and granddaughter carry your living remains, and that is the only thing that gives me comfort.

The wooden box that contains your ashes is on

the bookcase in the office where I can look at it. You'd like being carried in recycled pine beetle wood. We talked a lot about pine beetle wood on our trips to walk a labyrinth at Winfield in the Okanagan. We didn't know what we were talking about.

We didn't know. That's what you said in the hospital on about the fifth day, when things were happening so suddenly, so fatefully.

Morning and night, I weep and weep, weep and weep. You would have hated this weeping. Your dog Victor doesn't much like it either. People have suggested I must be feeling angry, but I haven't felt anger yet. Maybe I won't. I'm happy that you were healthy and active right up to the end of your life and that your dying wasn't prolonged. And I'm pleased to be able to tidy things up, bring order to the end of your life. I can't say I have done a lot of that, but I'm happy that you won't have to deal with these things. I'm glad you lived your life freely, exuberantly, irresponsibly, in a way that made you loved by everyone. I was glad that you were just who you were. Someone said that's what love is.

The pine beetle box is surprisingly light, surprisingly heavy. And what does it all mean, these remains of your days? And the remains of mine? *Leftover Life to Kill* is the title Caitlin Thomas gave to the book she wrote after Dylan's death. In Samuel Beckett's words, *I can't go on. I'll go on.*

Here's how it goes at the Hospice House Reiki session:

"Do I have permission to touch you?" the woman asks.

"At the hospital they didn't touch me," I say. That was three weeks ago. They moved their hands above me without touching.

"We normally start at the head and move slowly down the body with a very light touch. But if my touching makes you uncomfortable, signal and I'll stop."

Reiki is not my sort of thing, but I am in a different universe these days. The world has changed, I wrote on the subject line, emailing an old friend. He deleted my message unopened, assuming, reasonably enough, that it was spam. It felt like spam to me too.

This is my first private Reiki session, and I wouldn't have come if I'd thought they would actually touch me. But now I'm lying on the bed with pillows under my head and knees, the lights dim, massage-appropriate music playing. It would be rude to get up and go.

The Reiki woman's hands are on my forehead and I feel tears coming. Bad enough to be lying here so helplessly, but tears? My doctor suggested that I consider counselling. But grief counselling, you always said, is one of the evils of our time, along with orange safety vests for climbing up on a roof. Along with *Do Not Eat* warnings on houseplants, and car alarms that go off unnecessarily.

This is not grief counselling, Mike. It's a Reiki treatment. A spiritual practice designed to promote healing. You yourself had Reiki on the palliative care ward. When the Hospice workers came around, I agreed to let them do it because you'd been agitated and because it didn't involve touch. I volunteered to have the Reiki treatment myself at the same time. I thought it only fair. They even did dog Reiki on Victor. I asked the palliative care doctor what he thought about Reiki and he said, "I don't believe in it, but it seems to help."

And it did seem to help. I felt slightly more relaxed after my treatment. After his, Victor fell asleep. You were calmer too, and then you began to move your arms about slowly and gracefully, in long, looping gestures. The radio was playing the Correlli sonata you loved so much.

Correlli's name was Arcangelo. An archangel?

Like Michael. Sword of God, you used to say. One of the chief princes.

Are you conducting an orchestra, I asked, watching your arms loop back and forth.

Maybe, you said.

I drove to the park and sat in the car, listening to the river, and it came to me. You were dancing! Your long arms so beautiful and supple, so right for the music, your face serene. I raced back to the hospital and found you awake but now still, motionless.

You were dancing, weren't you?

Maybe, you said again.

The Reiki practitioner puts one hand under my head and the other moves slowly over my skull. Her hands are surprisingly hot. Not warm, but hot. Is this the energetic connection?

Ridiculous to be lying here at the Hospice program, this kindly woman's hands touching me, while you lie dead. Lie nowhere. While you are no longer you, but ashes in a box made of pine beetle wood on a bookcase in my office. How could we not have known when we drove through the Okanagan and saw the devastation caused by the pine beetles that some of that wood was going to be the material that contained your ashes?

It was all so fast. The ambulance, the brain scan, the spinal tap, more scans, more tests, no hope, palliative care, and you dead, seventeen days later.

We didn't know, you said, out of the blue.

Everything, everything, out of the blue.

I don't want to weep on the Reiki table so try to make my mind a blank. I envision the colour blue, a deep maritime blue, which shifts into cornflower blue and then a lighter greenish blue, the cover of my Ariadne book. Remember how long we spent looking at shades of blue to get the colour right? But, no, I can't think of that. I need to stay with the colour, not the memories. Cerulean shifts to indigo and I concentrate on pulling it back to the other colour. Ariadne blue.

Maybe I can hold back tears if I think of the times when you were less than good. There were plenty of those. My heart recoils to remember you turning and walking straight to your desk when I told you I had cancer. And little things too. How you wouldn't let me use your pens, even though you had dozens of them. How you said *shhhh, shhhh*, I'm thinking, when I wanted to talk about the Mediterranean Sea below us as we flew to Tel Aviv. That was a blue worth noting, the sparkling waters lapping up on those old Israeli shores.

It could have been different if I'd understood those moments when you needed to be alone in your own mind. When we first lived together you tacked a note above your desk that said *He who lives in his mind alone is happy.* I never knew whether that meant he who lived only in his mind was happy, or that he who lived in his mind was the only happy person.

Control. I've got to get control of my mind. The colour blue.

The natural blue of Mr. Koko's chiton shell eyes was close to Ariadne blue. Creating Mr. Koko took you a whole summer fifteen years ago. You dragged a log up from the beach to our deck and filled the kitchen with shells and stones and branches until you had everything in order to assemble your creation. Mr. Koko still stands on the porch of our island home. You said he protected us from bad spirits. He did that for a while, but even Mr. Koko couldn't hold death at bay forever.

Think of the word *bay*. Our little bay on Protection Island. Me, baying at the universe.

Think of your fetish. Mr. Koko. What was it with fetishes? Your many obsessions?

I used to joke about your pens, the way you were always searching for a better one, acquiring every new roller ball pen you could find. You carried several in your briefcase and always had two or three in your pockets. I found a box of pens, maybe two dozen, neatly lying side by side, row on row, on a high shelf in your clothes cupboard.

And the eyeglasses: more than three dozen pairs at last count, and never quite right. One on your nose, another hanging on a string around your neck. There were glasses in your briefcase, in drawers, on the counter, but they were never the ones you wanted at that moment.

Nail clippers, combs, notebooks. Photographs, letters, old programs. Shoes. Shirts. So many collections.

Reading Redmond O'Hanlon's *Back to Borneo,* you decided to make a fetish. I wrote about it in an article published by *the National Post*: Mr. Koko keeps Plague and Pestilence at Bay. You liked the article, and later you too wrote about Mr. Koko in one of the notebooks I found tucked away in your desk. Not the Mr. Koko that you created, but Koko as he created himself:

Koko rolled in the ocean, snorted like a porpoise, snored like a grampus, wise as a grandpa. He rode the ocean and rolled in the dips and crests of the sea. Singular, a log alone.

The sun cast light on the blond yellow cedar. Wind stirred splintered hair. Koko rolled ashore, beyond the barnacles, stranded himself on the shingle beach and waited while the tide dropped.

Koko cut himself to length, lay waiting for his feet to find him. His feet were a piece of common board, attached squarely to his log base. He took himself to a grassy hill, arranged his long tanned body for the axe, the chisels, the drawknife, the grinding block and grit paper. Maneuvered into a working place, he ground into himself the deep sockets of his eyes and the valley of a mouth, a deep, carmine red. His nose was chiseled from a groove high in his head, narrow and commanding. His long, pale arms were slim branches, washed in from Snake Island. Children came with teeth: shells, miniature conch or dentalium shells and the curved canines of a wolf from the Bowron Lakes.

Two chiton shells were brought to him and placed into the empty sockets. Koko looked out on the world, blue-eyed and sentient. Birds attacked, and his blunt glance drove them away.

Yesterday I noticed that one of Mr. Koko's blue eyes was gone. He stared at me, one-eyed and baleful. The empty socket seemed an accusation. Should we not have given the Eye Bank your eyes so that others could regain sight from the transplant of your cornea? Lying on this table, I cannot let myself think about that. At first the chiton shells were a light blue, but when they faded I painted them with a bright blue nail polish that has now softened to something closer to Ariadne blue.

Probably a crow. Crows are thieves and collectors, and blue attracts them. I'd rather imagine a bowerbird. We once had a painting of the Australian blue bowerbird, staring out from his nest festooned with blue objects: a toothbrush, a clothes peg, a straw, a button. I love the image, the bird looking out from his nest with only one thought: *blue, blue, the colour blue.*

The Reiki woman's hands move down my arms

now. I try to clear my mind of all thoughts and focus on the exact shade of blue. It is only through this sort of precision that I can begin to understand what grief is, what it means.

I am overcome with sadness about the absence of your presence. But that's self-pity. That is about me, what I've lost, not about you. When I focus on Ariadne blue, when I get control of that colour and hold it in my mind, for a moment I can experience pure grief. I concentrate on the colour of the sky we loved in a poster from the Shaw Festival, a huge sky that was blue as blue. But it keeps slipping away. Robin's egg blue, cerulean blue. I will start to cry again if I don't get control. Ariadne blue. Ariadne blue. I fix on it as Rosetti fixed on the woodspurge.

Carol is blue today and I never know what to do about it, you wrote in one of your journals.

Blue Moon was the song we danced to that first summer together at a little bar up in the Laurentians. So many songs: *Little Girl Blue, My Blue Heaven, Am I Blue. Mood Indigo.* All the blues.

Alexander Theroux in his book *The Primary Colours* proposes that blue might be "not so much a color as a state of mind." It's a mental state I try to conjure up from the memory of a Stratford sky, the quick flash of a kingfisher, or the darkened blue of a long night. It's the tone that Duke Ellington captured in *Mood Indigo*.

Long ago I read about myth as a cross: a vertical line representing life and death; a horizontal line representing animal and human. The quadrant of the living human connects with the quadrant of the dead animal and vice versa. I don't quite know what that means, but it seems to relate to you and Mr. Koko, and your animistic writing about shoes and shirts. The way you saw things:

> *Light on the water, rain*
> *in the grass, bluejay*
> *on the hedge.*
> *Every day*
> *is new.*
> *Each day is new,*
> *if we just knew.*

Maggots, maggots, maggots, you wrote in the last of your journal entries. *Mr. Koko looks at the world around him. Mr. Koko sees.*

I can't ask you what to make of all this.

You up there making the sky blue.

Me down here, my feet held by hot hands.

I go over and over in my mind the many ways in which I could have been a better wife. I was too self-absorbed, too unaware. I should have found a way to save you. This feeling, I've learned, is common in a bereaved person. As du Maurier wrote in her essay:

> *Like Emily Bronte, one of my first reactions*

after the first bewildered fit of weeping, was to blame myself. I could have done more during the last illness. I should have observed, with deep awareness, the ominous signs. I should have known, the last week, the last days, that his eyes followed me with greater intensity, and instead of moving about the house on trivial business as I did, never left his side. How heartless, in retrospect, my last good night, when he murmured to me, "I can't sleep," and I kissed him and said, "You will darling, you will," and went from the room. Perhaps, if I had sat with him all night, the morning would have been otherwise.

We had a good day together, that last one before you went to the hospital. We went for a long drive and you told me that whatever road you had to take in life you would want to travel it with me. Over dinner at Saigon Kitchen, on what was to be our last evening out together, we talked about some of the good trips we'd made and planned our next holiday. To Montreal in the fall, and maybe on to London. As we drove home, you became confused and asked if I was sure we were going in the right direction. When we got home, you asked where we were. Inside, you wanted to go to bed but you kept turning in the wrong direction. *I want to go to that bedroom, not this one.* In retrospect, I realize that you probably thought we were on the island, not at our townhouse, but at the time I couldn't figure out why you were so adamant about wanting to go to the study, not the bedroom. I was startled by your confusion and anger. Finally, when you were settled in bed, I poured myself a glass of wine and sat down to answer emails.

Are you coming?

I'll be along in a little while.

That night I wrote in my journal that you were not well and I feared for us both. Later, when I finally went to bed, you were already asleep. I crawled in beside you, fell asleep, and then awoke in the darkness to hear you crying out from the floor where you'd fallen.

Lift me up. Lift me up, you said as I struggled to lift you to the bed. Lift me up. At last I managed to get you propped up on the edge of the mattress but not comfortably. You didn't want me to call the ambulance, but finally I had to.

How I wish I'd gone to you when you called out earlier. Maybe you would have told me what was happening. Perhaps things might have gone differently.

Weeks later, I'm trying hard to do everything that you would want. Keep things in order, do household business, paperwork. Every day I make a point of going out, even if it's just to the store to pick up odds and ends—frames for photos of you, picture hangers, treats for Victor. I wear the scarf I knitted for you last year. You would like to see how well it matches my purple jacket. I try to imagine that it's like having your arms around me, but it doesn't really feel like that.

I was busy today and hardly cried. I cleared out the fridge and gave your frozen gyozas to friends who'd invited me for dinner. I knew I'd never eat them myself and you'd be happy to have them going to a good home. Now I'm drinking scotch and eating one of the chocolate macaroons I bought for you in that last week, remembering our conversation.

Eat, Hansel, I need to fatten you up.

I'm sorry, Gretel, I just can't do it.

There is no Gretel anymore, Hansel. It's just you and the old witch.

Don't say that!

If only I'd said that I was Gretel, that I'd always be with you and would find a way for us to escape, to get out of the woods. If only. The French have a nice expression for the ideas that come too late, the responses we wish we'd made. *L'esprit d'escalier.* The staircase spirit. You would like that expression.

I shouldn't be eating these macaroons. I don't need to fatten myself up, but I feel I'm taking in something of you. I grasp at any connection.

Spring is coming. Buds everywhere. Things blossoming. You dead. A friend came this afternoon to walk Victor and asked how I was doing. *Does it make you furious to see things blooming, the world coming to life all around you?*

No. No, it doesn't.

I could have explained that my sorrow is larger than springtime, beyond all blossoming. That I lack the heart to feel anger.

She says she's going to create a ritual for you on a Tofino beach. Something to do with pie. She said you and she talked about pies and exchanged pie recipes, but I pointed out that you never used recipes. She acknowledged this was true, but said you'd told her how you made your pies. I get resentful of people when they claim intimacy with you. I want to keep it just for me, and so I am sometimes cool in response to the sadness of others, although I know their feelings are genuine.

Another friend phoned to ask how I was and I told her the truth. I said I was desolate and life would never be as good for me again, that there would not ever again be the joy I've had with you. She agreed. I appreciated that.

It's summer now and I take Victor to the dog park every afternoon. I watch him, a white dog sprawled out in a patch of sunlight on the green grass. Eyes closed, almost asleep, he is panting from the heat.

He could move into the surrounding shade under the tall evergreen trees, but he chooses to stay where he is and pant in the sunlight.

Am I like that, preferring my grief to whatever solace might be available? I want to avoid what is maudlin and sentimental. I want to stay with what is real. Perhaps Victor sees the sunshine as real, no matter how uncomfortable.

A few days ago I dreamt I was alone in a strange building and there were sounds of people in other rooms, some shouting, some crying. A feeling of chaos and uncertainty overwhelmed me and then I realized that there was someone in the bed with me. I asked, *Who are you?* and you turned towards me, with a sweet, pleased smile. *It's Mike*, you answered. I was filled with joy when I awoke.

In another dream, we were in a large hotel, attending an important conference. There were many corridors, twists and turns. Unexpectedly you turned a corner and I didn't know where you were. I called your name and the sound of my own voice awakened me.

Last night you appeared in a dream proposing that we could go to Africa to teach a course. I worried about the living conditions. I asked our niece who said two things: yes, it would be challenging, and that may be just why we'd want to consider it. You headed off somewhere, keen to leave, checking out travel possibilities, but later you were in bed with me, your head on the pillow next to me and I asked you questions. *What's ahead?* When I awoke, you weren't beside me and I called your name aloud before I realized that you are, of course, dead. Dead!

In the most surprising dream I was travelling with you and a young boy in a small boat on a lake. We were all facing forward, the boy in front, me behind him, and you at the rear. Suddenly I realized you were no longer steering the boat. I looked behind and saw that you were in the water, face down. I picked up the oars and started to row, calling for help but nobody responded. When I got to shore, others were looking on, all accepting that you were dead. Somehow I managed to carry your limp body to the doors of a nearby hospital and the doctor confirmed your death. Since we were in a foreign country, there were legalities to negotiate, forms to fill out. I didn't know where to go, what to do, but I realized the young boy was still with me and that was a comfort.

You'd be impressed with the way I cope. The garbage, the recycling, the lock on the gate to the park, the dog walks, the grocery shopping. I've changed the cartridges in the printer, albeit with some effort, and I've also managed to open difficult bottles. You liked to make a big show of your muscular superiority, very slowly twisting and twisting a bottle lid, saying, *There you are, little lady. At your service.*

I hate doing such things. I want you here doing them for me. I want you here doing anything, or nothing at all. I even want you back in the hospital, in palliative care. At least then I could be close to you.

I'd give anything to feel your presence, but the nearest I come is in the sudden expectation that you might at this very moment be coming through the door, that I might feel your hands on my shoulders, hear your voice proposing that we have a *cuppa*, or a *nipperkin*, or a *kippo*. I can almost imagine it for an instant before realizing that I'll never hear those words again. Nobody else will call me *Kettle* or *Peaches*.

Most of all I miss talking to you about everything. An old friend of ours wrote,

> *You guys were such devoted friends and your talk was the lifeblood and grist of your relationship. To have that conversation silenced has to leave you bereft, for what is there to replace it?*

Nothing. And nothing will come of nothing.

Never again to drink your powerful coffee: *There is no such thing as coffee that is too strong, only people who are too weak.* Never to watch you across the table from me having a *squinto* at the newspaper, offering to read me a little tidbit. Never again the familiar gestures, the laugh I loved. Never the afternoon nap.

I am an amputee who has lost the best part of herself.

Now all I have is a series of images that come

to me in an endless loop: you lying on the floor, saying *Lift me up, lift me up.* You in the medical ward holding earphones to your head, listening to Mozart on the DVD player, tears in your eyes, saying, *It lifts me... the music lifts me.* You sitting on the edge of your hospital bed, trying to get up to walk with the activity aide and saying, *Shit, shit, shit, shit, shit,* because the message will not get from your brain to your legs. Later, enraged, saying, *What's this weeping about? Your job is to look after her!* Jabbing a finger towards Alison. You, puzzled, shaking your head, *We didn't know, we didn't know.*

I now know, but you know nothing about what's going on in my life. It would be so good to think you're looking down on me, proud of how I'm carrying on, prevailing, but I can't believe that.

It's been almost a year. *You're doing really well,* people say to me now. Well? What do they mean? What do they see? Not what's inside of me. Not how I am when I'm alone.

Some years back, at the reception after the memorial service for her husband, a bereaved friend turned to us as we were leaving and said, *Now it's time for me to go and join the widows.* She gestured towards a group of three women who were also recently bereaved. There was an aura of apartness about these women, a kind of bleak bravado. Sad, but determined. Bloody but unbowed.

Plucky. The image stays with me.

The widows. The look of them. The sound of them. Of the word. Merry, black, or recently bereaved, *widow* has a sinister sound.

And *widowhood*. Something cloaked. Something hidden.

Although I too am now bereaved, I reject widowhood. I refuse to think of myself as a widow. You are dead, but I'm still married to you. I don't think of you as my late husband. In point of fact, I was the one who was always late. You were happy to be at the tarmac an hour before the ferry was due to leave, to be sitting at the theatre long before the curtain rose. You would jump from a train two or three stations too soon. That's why we called you "The Bolter." It was how you lived and left your life. Too early. Too fast. Too soon.

During the last week before you were taken to hospital, I played a lot of online Solitaire. You would look over my shoulder and ask what I was doing and I'd say *I'm sorry, sorry. I'm stupidly addicted to this. I'll just be a moment.* You'd turn away and say, *It's all right. You're under a lot of stress.*

It was true. I was under a lot of stress, although I don't think I had a name for it. I was worried, anxious, numb with apprehension. If I'd been more aware I would have spent every second of my day talking with you, not trying to divert myself with a foolish card game.

Well, now I play Solitaire several times a day

without interruption. I've made it up to 44%. That's out of 2,928 games. Perhaps I'm learning how to be solitary?

Come to me in my dreams, and then
By day I shall be well again!
For so the night will more than pay
The hopeless longing of the day.

Longing, *Matthew Arnold*

Longing

August, 1962. You are framed in the entrance to the Ladies and Escorts side at the Georgia Pub. Tall, slim, muscular and tanned, you're wearing a short-sleeved, red-and-white checked shirt and narrow blue jeans. Your eyes are hazel, greyish green, and you have a Van Dyke beard that strikes me at once as distinguished and bohemian. There's an old saying that love is blind, yet if there is a similarity between that courtship phase and my bereavement it's in the clarity and detail with which I saw you then and do again now.

You were twenty-five years old. I was nineteen. Not legally of age to be in a pub, but I looked older and had false identification. My friend spotted you and your friend over on the Men's side. In those days, men couldn't enter the Ladies and Escorts side unless they were with a woman, so she paged you, then told the waiter we expected two men to join us. I knew you by sight and reputation—a heartbreakingly handsome poet with a regular column in the UBC newspaper and a reputation as an "angry young man"—so I was thrilled to be actually sitting across the table from you.

At the time, it felt historic. It was historic.

You'd just returned to Vancouver from a summer at Bralorne. *It must be exciting, working in a gold mine*, I said, which made you laugh.

It was hell, you said. *Every day I put on the regulation gear and plummeted a mile below sea level where everything was dark and warm. At night we went to the miner's bar in the local hotel. That was it.* You were elated to be above ground and back in a city. I wanted to ask more about the gold mine, the actual work of it, but was too shy, intimidated by your intelligence, your wit.

When I told you I was planning to leave Vancouver for Montreal, you admired my decision. *No reason to stay in Vancouver*, you declared, and immediately quoted Malcolm Lowry's description of the construction of Vancouver, named Enochville in his story, *The Bravest Boat*, as a city made up of masonries, English tea shoppes, drapers' shops with opium dens in the basement. *But no bars*, you trumpeted, because *What would our wee laddies come to then?*

Our first outing alone was to a movie, *Barabbas*, not one that I would otherwise have gone to see.

You had a huge appetite for every new film, from Bergman to *Barabbas*, and strong opinions about each of them. I saw from the refreshments you carried into the theatre that you had a large appetite for food as well: two large paper bags filled with chicken wings, sausage rolls, Cornish pasties, potato chips, dill pickles, large bottles of Coke and Seven-up, and a couple of chocolate bars.

It's going to be a long movie, you explained.

The people around us were probably as surprised as I by the endless treats you pulled out of these bags but, like me, they said nothing. We munched through scenes of Anthony Quinn as brutish Barabbas, who'd also spent a good deal of time in the mines before becoming a gladiator and splashing blood around in grisly gladiatorial adventures. We chewed away while the spiritual Silvana Mangano spread the teachings of Christ, and Katy Jurado got stoned to death. Afterwards, we agreed that it wasn't a good movie, but we both liked Jack Palance, the very wickedest of gladiators. And we liked each other.

We met a couple of times a week for the next several months and went together to plays, concert, movies and poetry readings. When we were apart, I yearned for you. Often girls from the university hung around you, girls I thought much prettier than I, and I felt jealous, even though you appeared indifferent to their attentions. I had quit school to work as a clerk in an insurance office and, although I liked my work in what I thought of as the real world, I was worried that you might find me ignorant and inferior to your university companions.

I told you about how I planned to travel and was getting up early in the mornings to read European novels and teach myself Greek. *Aha,* you said, *you're an autodidact,* and explained that, while you thought that admirable, it was very useful to have an academic framework in order to learn what you didn't know. I learned a lot from you during those early days and listened closely as you explained things to me. You described how the most interesting poetry was now being written on the West Coast, in BC and in California, not in the East or in Europe. You told me about the Black Mountain poets and spoke at length about the brilliance of Robert Creeley.

All your views were completely new to me. I was fascinated, riveted and speechless with admiration, I bought every book you recommended and listened to whatever kind of music you said you liked. Years later you sometimes recalled, *I really enjoyed it when you just sat quietly and listened to everything I had to say, Couldn't you try to do a bit more of that now?*

On our first real date, you took me for dinner at a steak house, a candlelit dinner in a fancy restaurant. You ordered the Chateaubriand with a wine and shallot sauce. I wasn't much of a meat eater, but I wanted to do anything you suggested.

When the waiter asked how we'd like our steak you said, *Very rare* at the moment that I asked for *Very well done*, not knowing that this would be one serving for both of us. You then insisted that medium would be good, the first of many compromises.

I liked walking beside you, feeling the comfortable physicality of your presence. The expression *bien dans sa peau* described you. Once, in a bar, a man made an advance towards me and you waved him off with a cheerful authority that made me think I'd always be safe with you.

When I left for Montreal you gave me a copy of Creeley's *For Love* to read on the bus. That afternoon I'd gone to UBC to hear a poetry reading at which you were one of three poets who read. Fred Wah was inspiring, especially when he sang part of one poem, and Lionel Kearns intrigued me with his "stacked verse" and quixotic subjects. You were the best. The cleverest, most witty, most original. After the reading, we had dinner at my parents' home and you came along to say goodbye when they drove me to the bus depot.

Truth be told, I was besotted with you. If you'd asked me then to stay, I might never have left. And, if so, how would things have turned out?

I'm now sorting through a large file of the letters I wrote to you from Montreal, fifty years ago. You saved them all, folded back into their envelopes. As I read these letters, I ache for you as I did then. A hopeless longing and a precise one.

My first letter was from a bus station in Regina in February of 1963. It says, *I'd like to phone you but am sure you'll be out.* I'd hardly left Vancouver and was already missing you. In several letters, I tried to make my fellow passengers sound comic or sinister. I described a middle-aged lady who carried several paper bags and got sick into them. In an attempt to make you jealous, I wrote about two whispering gangsters who liked me because at their request I sang songs their mothers had taught them. What pleased you most was my description of

> *a garrulous old man named Guy who told stories about his wife, Spider, that made her blush. "Oh, Guy," she would murmur, "that's not true," while he bragged about what a good wife she was: "Every time I put my feet under the table, Spider put something good to eat on top of it."*

You kept all my letters and remembered those descriptions, and years later sometimes referred to us as "Spider" and "Guy." They were figures of married contentment, like Darby and Joan, who were *"dropsical and sore-eyed"* yet never happy asunder.

Longing and loneliness are often intertwined. The desire for the unattainable increases the sense of aloneness, and vice versa. My letters from Montreal describe frequent episodes of intense loneliness and after only a few weeks away I proposed that you should take a leave of absence from your job and fly out to visit me: *The bus fare is only $42 and you could get a room where I am for $9.00 a week.* I wrote about the free concerts, Instant Theatre's one-act, lunch-hour plays at Place Ville Marie for 65 cents, the lecture series I was attending.

I don't have the letters you wrote back to me during those early months. Sometime the following year I lost all the papers I'd carried from room to room. I know now that you must have written several times because many of my letters thank you for yours.

Reading these letters I relive my longing for you. The way I felt then was not unlike the way I feel now, but the desire now is even greater, more intense. At the time I felt brave being on my own, but it requires much more bravery to be alone now. To have had and to have lost you.

Our letters sustained me through those lonely months. You were wise and witty, if often a bit distant. Not just in the sense of the three thousand miles that separated us, but in the sense of being preoccupied, of having your attention elsewhere. Yet at least once you must have said something about marriage, because there's a letter from me in which I say that I've read your statement that you had more than once thought of coming to Montreal to ask me to marry you. It was slighting, I thought, that you had more than once dismissed such an idea. I wrote back to say that one rejection I could ignore, but more than one?

At that time I was beginning to get involved with another man and about to become engaged, but my letters don't mention him. We continued to write to each other, though less frequently, until finally our letters tapered off by the end of the year, when you had, I think, fallen in love with someone else. There were bad months ahead for both of us—broken relationships, broken hearts, unemployment, and a general sense of disappointment and discontent. We wrote nothing for over a year.

I was the first to write again. You'd never really been out of my mind during those absent months, but I wasn't proud of how I'd let my life fall apart. I'd been out of work, living a dissolute life—drinking, not working, in and out of relationships, with no sense of responsibility for myself or anyone else. In the beginning, I was afraid you'd want nothing to do with me in the state I was in.

My first letter begins on August 13th, 1964, breaks off until August 27th and is finally completed on August 31st. It describes the ups and downs of my life, an uncertain emotional state, a suicide attempt, psychiatric sessions, and ends with the plea, *Will you write me something, please?*

When you reply, I respond immediately. Again I propose that you should move to Montreal where you could work at the McGill library, do some acting, get some TV parts, drink in nice taverns and buy good, cheap, imported wine. I write letter after letter, saying how important our correspondence is to me:

Somehow I feel I have a sort of direction with you which must be because of the inner solidity that you have. I should be working, but all I want to do is to write to you.

Surprisingly, you write back in a similar vein:

I have two letters from you to answer—it's not some vague and abstract formality, some punctilio, that makes me want to reply immediately, even though I don't, but just the fact that I like talking to you… I'm a clodhopper. I might at least press some flowers (it's spring and full of gorgeous smells in the air) and send them for you. Take the thought for the deed, take the word for the touch…

And later:

Dear Carol, I want to be with you. "To prune these growing plants, and tend these flowers which were it toilsome yet with thee were sweet."

We'd both come to realize how much we meant to each other and, after the long silence, we quickly moved to a new level of intimacy. Now, when I go over them I can see how healing your letters were. In my own, I try to impress you with the ways in which I'd changed and matured, and with the new directions I was pursuing: becoming more fluent in French, joining a choir, learning to play the organ. I knew you'd admire my taking up the organ. Years earlier you'd sometimes gone to the Kerrisdale Presbyterian Church, which I'd attended as a child. I remember seeing you there when I was eleven, singing in the choir. You were in the back row with a group of sixteen-year-old boys who'd been coerced to attend after playing basketball in the church hall. You were famously good-looking.

Our letters grew more and more frequent and the longing to meet in person became more passionate. Yet I began to worry that you'd be disappointed with me when we actually met again:

> *I think about it so much that I have to stop and tell myself that it doesn't matter, it doesn't matter, it doesn't matter at all. And I'm not quite sure what I mean by this or why I say it. Because it does matter. It matters more than anything.*

You reassure me:

> *You don't have to feel that I am counting on you, throwing any kind of obligation at*

you—just know that I am anticipating you. I
have no suspicions about your sanity; you sound
more in contact with a real, a vital reality than
about anyone I know … I remember you as
someone who was always, no matter where, or
who you were with, someone who couldn't,
inside at least, be pushed around. What all
that clumsiness means is that I think you
have the kind of honesty or integrity that I call
character.

I still find your opinion of me too positive:

Are you sure you actually really remember
me? It isn't that I don't think I'm worthwhile—
I may be—but I don't know how you could ever
have known.

We both write about the need to meet again and
you are annoyed when I say that I'll have to delay
my trip to Vancouver because my psychoanalyst
wants me to take holidays only during the time
that she will also be away.

Why must you return to Montreal to accord
with the movements of your psychiatrist? (a
personage, by the way, that I will probably want
you to get rid of.) I realize that such an attitude
is stupid and unfair, but while my habit is to
be the sweetest and most pliable of creatures, my
impulses are to be selfish and unreasonable.

I jokingly question your wanting to interfere with the delicate therapeutic relationship and point out that the doctor I am now seeing is actually psychoanalyst and not a mere therapist, which represents a big financial and prestige difference, but in the letters that follow I say:

> I don't want to see my doctor any more...
> I'm bored with talking about myself, wish she
> would contribute something to the conversation.
> It's an unnatural social situation and no
> normal person would deal with it.

Clearly your letters are becoming much more therapeutic than my daily sessions in analysis. Therapy is abstract and meaningless in contrast to our correspondence. Analysis seems artificial and hypothetical, whereas I feel that you talk about real life, as when you write:

> It's frightening how clear is the division
> between meaningful work and just shuffling
> around, wasting time, paying the rent, hating
> the neighbours, hating people in general. And
> this hating people—it must invariably go with
> making nothing of yourself—because to make
> anything of yourself means losing yourself in
> other people—whether in service, or in just
> loving or seeing friends. I honestly don't know
> if I'm a worthwhile person, but I would walk
> a mile to do anyone a favour, a service—as

long as I respected them and the favour they wanted, and I might feel big about doing it to—but why shouldn't I? I take the same pride in being good to people, whenever I'm able to, that I would take in any job I could do well. Feeling humble, being self-abnegating is a recent invention. The Greeks were proud of everything they did; they either thumped their chests or wept with shame. Because they cared about things enough to. They weren't being self-centred or self-dramatizing. They cared more. They lived harder.

Your letters give me strength and I write that I'm aware of a sort of awakening and unfolding, always, with you.

The French word is epanouissement, I say and add, embarrassed, *Isn't that impressive, my not being able to find the English equivalent?*

And later I report:

An Estonian girl I work with tells me that when she first came to Canada, not speaking any English, she used to simply copy sounds that people made, and for years was saying, 'Our Father, who art in heaven, how did you know my name?' For some reason this breaks me up, Mike. But that is how I feel about you... how did you know?

As soon as I arrive in Vancouver for my two-week vacation, you tell me you are planning to leave your job and come to join me in Montreal.

I have all the letters we wrote to each other after I returned to Montreal. On my first day back I found an apartment for us. I was excited about the location:

> It's in an old brick building in Westmount. The balcony looks out on a nicely treed street. There's a sunroof and two big bedrooms! We could have fights and then sleep in separate rooms! ... Hurry, hurry, hurry, hurry, hurry here. I am impatient for it all to begin.

You responded immediately:

> My eyes bugged out of my head and I turned cartwheels when I opened your letter. All said I think it's the greatest letter I ever read in my life.

We both wrote frequently throughout that month, our letters complaining about how slowly time was moving, you wrote:

> I am dying to get to you... I hope I am not just a dull little guy with a beard. I hope I can make you happy.

Now, fifty years later, I am reading through these early letters and also the many letters we exchanged during the six weeks when I first came to Nanaimo to find a home for us while you remained in Montreal, teaching a summer class and working on your thesis. I have dozens of notes and cards and poems written throughout our forty-six and a half years of marriage. And there's a log you kept for me each day when, just after I retired, I went to Montreal for a week alone. We'd been married for thirty-five years then and were hardly ever apart. When I came home, you gave me the *Log of Michael P. Hog* in which you kept track of events during my absence. You closed it saying

I want you to realize that I don't just miss you as something lacking in my life when you're gone, but also as a positive inspiration. I just feel more alive and facing forward when you are at hand.

I keep looking at your notebooks and diaries. I pore over them, trying to know exactly what you were thinking, wanting to understand, wishing I could ask you questions. Everything about you is again mysterious and remarkable and fascinating.

Over the next while, I think I'll come to know you better than ever before. I'll understand who you truly are and who I am, now that neither of us is as we were. And I'll long for you more than ever. Reading your old letters, I recall the exuberant young man you were when we first met, and I long for him. A boy, really. And that boy never really left you, did he? *Why don't you grow up?* I would ask in later years, irritated by what I saw as stubborn irrespon- sibility. And you'd talk about Wordsworth and about the child being father to the man, *trailing clouds of glory*, and so forth.

After you died, I dreamt again about the boy who was with us in a boat and who stayed with me when I carried your dead body to the hospital. That part of you stays with me. The boy.

In the wee, small hours of the morning... I think about the boy.

Now I understand what it is to really long for someone. The longing, the sense of distance and desire. From Old English *langun*, often defined as a persistent craving for something unattainable, which pretty much sums it up. Sometimes equated with weariness and dejection, says my dictionary.

A regular favourite in our family singsongs when I was a child was that 19th century parlour song: *Just A-Wearyin' for you, All the time a-feelin' blue...*

That's how it is with me, Mike. *All the time a-feelin' blue.*

Time after time. On one of our early outings, I asked why you didn't wear a watch, and you produced an old-fashioned timepiece from your trouser pocket, saying, *I carry time in my pocket, not strapped to my body!* And now you and that pocket of time have disappeared.

It's agonizing to be going over old memories all by myself, to be longing for you now just as I did in those early years, but with no hope of satisfaction. I remind myself of what Rumi said:

Longing is the core of mystery. Longing itself brings the cure. The only rule is, suffer the pain.

Believe me, I am longing. I am suffering the pain.

The secret of marriage is that of religion itself: the emergence of the larger self, and the finding of one's life by the losing of it. From the separateness of your individual lives, you have come together to build a single life. From the privacy of your separate worlds, you have come to share a single world. Separately, you were bound by the limits of your individual being; together you have entered a wider realm of being, made open to you by the merging of your separate lives into a larger whole.

Our marriage ceremony,
Reverend Robert Gardiner

Belonging

November 6, 1965. We'd heard that marriage under Quebec's Napoleonic Code required a contract and thought, mistakenly, that this would not be applicable if we married in the States so we decided to get married at the home of my brother and sister-in-law in Wellesley, Massachusetts. But, after we'd done the blood tests for venereal disease, which were required in those days, and bought the marriage license, we found out that we couldn't be married in a civil ceremony in Wellesley. In Wellesley, we were told, people are married in churches.

At the last moment, my brother persuaded the Chaplain at M.I.T. to marry us. I met Rev. Gardiner the night before the wedding, at which time you were already heading toward me on a bus from Montreal, my gold wedding ring on a ribbon around your neck.

Have you written your ceremony? Rev. Gardiner

asked, and I mumbled that it hadn't occurred to us to do that.

I prefer couples to create their own ceremony. Ah well, there's not much time, is there? How much theology do you want?

I hesitated, not sure how one should respond to that question when asked by a clergyman.

God talk, God talk, he explained.

I guess it wouldn't mean a lot to us.

That's how I feel... I prefer Martin Buber. I, Thou, you know...

I told him we'd thought of poems we liked and asked if he would read Shakespeare's Sonnet 116:

Let me not to the marriage of true minds
Admit impediments.
Love is not love
Which alters when it alteration finds,
Or bends with the remover to remove:
O no! it is an ever-fixed mark
That looks on tempests and is never shaken;
It is the star to every wandering bark,
Whose worth's unknown, although his height be taken.
Love's not Time's fool, though rosy lips and cheeks
Within his bending sickle's compass come:
Love alters not with his brief hours and weeks,
But bears it out even to the edge of doom.
If this be error and upon me proved,
I never writ, nor no man ever loved.

He asked if I was aware of speculation that the

sonnet had been written for another man.

I don't think that would concern us.

I just wondered if some of the wedding guests might be troubled.

I explained that we'd only have a few family members present and they'd be fine with it.

For our wedding ceremony you'd also suggested that "Prayer," a poem by George Herbert, be read:

Prayer the church's banquet, angel's age,
God's breath in man returning to his birth,
The soul in paraphrase, heart in pilgrimage,
The Christian plummet sounding heav'n and earth...

Exalted manna, gladness of the best,
Heaven in ordinary, man well drest,
The milky way, the bird of Paradise,
Church-bells beyond the stars heard, the soul's blood,
The land of spices; something understood.

Rev. Gardiner agreed it was a terrific poem but said the metaphysics were too complex. He would need at least a few weeks to get his head around it. I loved the imagery and language of that mystical prayer—*The soul in paraphrase, heart in pilgrimage*—but I could see what he meant, and we were proud of ourselves for having proposed such a challenging poem.

Until then we'd seen the wedding as only a perfunctory step, but it was more meaningful than we could have imagined. I was anxious and took two Elavils before the ceremony. In some photographs you appear to be propping me up, but Rev. Gardiner's words were so interesting that at a certain point I simply forgot to be nervous. Later we asked him for a copy of the ceremony and made a great many photocopies of it, circulating them to all our friends. Through the years we'd offer it up to engaged couples and much later gave it to Alison, who used some of it at her own wedding.

As I go through your files, I find that you kept several copies of that ceremony in various places. I read it again and again, recalling that unseasonably sunny November afternoon, the yellow roses on your lapel and on the brim of my big brown velvet hat. We stood for photographs in the garden, smiling and stylish, me in a champagne-coloured boucle suit and you in your new slim, charcoal suit. The photographs are black and white, now turned almost sepia, but my own view is full of colour, the bright fall leaves and the blue dresses of my mother and sister-in-law. My real life about to begin.

For our honeymoon we spent two days in Rockport, Maine, a small seaside town on Cape Ann, once an artist's colony, where we walked along the pier and admired the weathered, red fishing shack, which was painted so often it was referred to as Motif No.1. The setting was picturesque, but there was little to do and no place to drink, as Rockport was a dry town. A waitress told us that a hundred years earlier, a seventy-five-year-old spinster named Hannah Jumper had organized a group of almost two hundred women in the "War Against Demon Rum." Hannah and the Hatchet Gang stormed through town one night with tomahawks, hammers and hatchets and raided establishments where liquor was sold and emptied over fifty barrels of liquor on the street. After that the town voted for prohibition every year and was now one of only a few towns in the country that was dry.

We hopped on a train to Gloucester for dinner, at which we drank a lot of wine. You were excited to be in Charles Olson's town, the setting for his Maximus Poems. You wanted to have more time both here and in New York. We had our first married argument about that, walking back from the train to our lodgings, me insisting that we'd promised my brother that we would return and that we should see my mother before she took the train back to the West Coast, you saying this was a chance for us to do something memorable.

We had our second argument when we arrived at the Port Authority Bus Terminal in New York. The place was rushed and rough and we were tired and jangled. Excuse me, you said to a passerby, *Could you tell us how to get to...* , but the man was gone before you'd finished the question. Everyone around us was racing past and talking fast, so you wanted just to throw our suitcases into a locker and get ourselves out as quickly as we could, but I refused to leave without my nightgown and toothbrush. After some shrill shouting back and forth, we shouldered our bags and, with much trial and error, made our way to the subway, arriving at your friends' apartment on the Lower East Side less than an hour before the big 1965 power outage plunged the city into darkness and chaos. We wandered out on the streets amongst throngs of people walking home across the Brooklyn Bridge. I was thrilled to see the huge skyscrapers dimly lit with candles in their windows. Somehow that image feels fitting for what I'm doing in my life right now. Seeking tiny points of light within a huge surround of darkness and shadow. Searching for space and light.

C.S. Lewis was right in proposing that bereavement is a phase of marriage similar to the courtship. I've realized that my longing for you now is similar to the yearning I felt in those early days. But if bereavement is not a truncation of a marriage, I must think more about what it was to be married for almost 47 years.

I can see now that we truly did have the marriage of true minds. No matter how many other things went wrong, there was no alteration there. And it was a wonderful thing, that new realm, that larger circle in which we didn't distinguish the one from the other. Who was who and which was which no longer mattered. When, in a crowd of people I'd meet your gaze, I knew that we were thinking the same thought. Often one of us would say something and the other would reply, *That's just what I was thinking.*

I think you and Mike were lucky to find each other, my brother said to me shortly after you died.

What do you mean? You think nobody else would have had us?

No, he replied, patiently. *I just think you were lucky.*

I'd had a number of boyfriends and, although my mother once told me that I wasn't exactly an oil painting, quite a few men had found me attractive. Yet I wasn't confident that any man who wanted to marry me would be someone I'd actually want to marry. When I was very young, maybe seven years old, my music teacher had me sing a song at a concert that went like this:

> *If no one ever marries me,*
> *And I don't see why they should,*
> *For Nurse says I'm not pretty*
> *And I'm seldom very good,*
> *If no one ever marries me*
> *I shan't mind very much.*
> *I shall buy a squirrel in a cage*
> *And a little rabbit hutch.*

I didn't always think it, but I do now know how very lucky we were to find each other. Not everyone finds a partner with whom they are so well matched. After your death, several people commented on how complementary our partnership was. You were a compound noun—*Carol and Mike, we always spoke of you together,* said one friend. You were one, said a former colleague. *Inseparable.* We thought that too. *Cathected,* I would say, and sometimes suggested that we should try to do something about it.

You've lost your soulmate, people have said, and perhaps that is true. What I know for sure is that I've lost my mindmate. My best friend. The love of my life. And yet that closeness meant that, in our flaws and failures, we were also one. Sometimes I felt a sense of claustrophobia and suffocation and so, lashing out at myself, I would lash out at you. When I was angry or unhappy, it didn't matter how it came about, what it was about, or who had caused it; I directed my frustration towards you. There was no distinction between us in bad as well as in good times. Which meant that I often didn't see you as separate from me. In David Foster Wallace's memorable commencement speech he tells the story of two young fish meeting an older fish who says, "Morning, boys, how's the water?" And the two young fish are confused and finally ask, "What the hell is water?" Wallace uses this story to make the point that we don't see the obvious and important realities that are right around us. It is the dailiness of our lives, invisible then, that I miss now.

Now that you are dead, I experience you as apart. I see you as a separate being and experience again the I and Thou that our marriage was at its very best. For a while it was all water, but now I see you clearly and distinctly again, now that I have lost you forever.

Except... except... *love's not time's fool.* Our marriage is still a star, a compass, my wandering bark. Our marriage continues to the edge of doom, even in this bereavement phase, whatever it means. Past your doom, and on to mine.

Before we married you had promised me fun, and you delivered. My parents had taught me responsibility, and I rebelled against it. You taught me irresponsibility, and I reveled in it. We were both youngest children and we lacked the drive to achieve that was so evident in our brothers. *Eat, drink and be merry* was good enough for us, we said, and we did, we were. You showed me how to live a day at a time and not care for the future.

Our first Montreal home together was a two-bedroom unfurnished apartment in an old brick building on Claremont Avenue. Before that, I'd mostly lived in furnished rooms, but for this apartment I acquired a table and chairs, a sofa an old-fashioned standing lamp, and a couple of old carpets and, of course, the usual assortment of boards and bricks that served as bookcases. You arrived with two cast-iron frying pans, your record collection and a large, very beautiful, pale green ashtray by a Vancouver ceramicist named Tam Irwin. Some twenty boxes of books were being shipped out. *My dowry*, you bragged.

Those early years were magical. You worked at the McGill library and I worked at the hospital. I felt like someone in a college novel when I met you after work. We'd hang out at the Swiss Hut or listen to music at the Fifth Dimension, which later became the Fifth Amendment, and we'd talk and talk. On weekends, we walked up to Mount Royal or down to the Atwater Market. We brought home fresh vegetables, fruit, cheese and meat. You bought a big Dutch oven and took to cooking up enormous pots of chili, or stew, or *sauerbraten*, so large that we often had to invite friends in for dinners. Most nights, though, we preferred to be alone, just the two of us. There was so much to say.

You learned that, by taking only a few qualifying courses, you could get conditional admission to a Master's program at Sir George Williams University. Being married to a poor graduate student was romantic, I thought, and I was happy to type your papers for the next few years.

On our first Christmas together, you gave me a metal tackle box with a lock and key. You'd been dismayed when I told you that my mother often read my diary and insisted on seeing letters that my friends wrote. *This is just for your private papers,* you said. *You can keep it locked.* You also gave me a compass, because I had no sense of direction and frequently got lost. A compass, of course, doesn't actually help when you really have no sense of direction, but those two gifts made me feel that at last I had my own space and that, in my life with you, I knew where I was going.

After a year we moved to the McGill ghetto. Our apartment was on the top floor of an elegant old house on Ste. Famille. Below us lived Michel, a musician and composer, and Vanda, a ballerina with *Les Grand Ballets,* and on the ground floor was Gavin, a young architect who was to become a lifelong friend and unofficial godfather to our daughter. All around, creative people were doing good work. To the south were Quebecois jazz musicians who played late into the night, and to the north the Grey Nuns ran a kindergarten during the days. Gavin spent weeks creating enormous mobiles of circles of balsa wood painted in bright primary colours, climbing the back stairs to our balcony to hang them from the large maple tree in the back yard. We bought an old piano, on which a friend painted the name *Stradivarius* in golden, gothic script. While you studied, I practiced Bach's French suites.

It was the year of Expo 67, and the city was

full of life. Music and theatre were everywhere. One night, after watching an old Fred Astaire and Ginger Rogers movie on television, I said I wish we lived in a time when people jumped up on restaurant counters and sang and danced at the drop of a hat. *Shhh*, you said. Listen. Look. And sure enough we heard singing on the street. We went to the window and by the moonlight we could see Vanda doing *pirouette* and *pas de chats*, with Michel cantering beside to catch her as she leapt into the air.

After Vanda and Michel moved to a larger apartment, an intense young socialist moved into their flat and held classes for the Free University, often hosting them on the front stairs so that we had to step over young radicals. *Youth in Asia*, was one of the classes, which you referred to as *Euthanasia*, wondering why it wasn't used on those students.

Once or twice I dragged you up to Fletcher's Field for the love-ins that happened on weekends. *Why are those stoned young women saying, "Merry Christmas"?* you asked. *It's Hare Krishna,* I told you. Some of them are hugging little kittens, you observed. *I suspect they intend to cook them up for their dinners,* you speculated. You were not keen on love-ins, insisting that the fifties were in every way a superior decade to the decadent sixties.

We were beginning to tire of the area and so, when Gavin moved away, we decided to find a new location. We moved to a Sherbrooke Street apartment with a long hallway and a pumpkin-coloured living room, and soon after we moved I discovered I was pregnant. We hadn't discussed the possibility of having a child and certainly wouldn't have planned it until you'd finished your Master's degree. We'd gone away with friends for a weekend in Upstate New York and I'd forgotten my birth control pills. I was apprehensive about your reaction.

I suppose we could have it, you said, thoughtfully, after a few silent moments. What was the alternative? But very soon you became enthusiastic about the prospect, boasting about the great things you would do with your son. Nicholas.

Me and Nick will go off to the basketball hoop down the road... and one day I'll teach him how to fish. Many sentences began, *My son and I...*

Once I asked, *What if it's a girl?* and you quickly replied, *We could put her in the Dutch oven and roast her up for a great big dinner.* I thought it was not the proper thing to say to a pregnant woman, but as soon as our daughter was born you burst into my hospital room, crowing about her intelligent cry compared to the other babies who seemed *foolishly placid.*

You're not disappointed? I asked.

What are you talking about?

A girl. Not a son. Not Nicholas.

A son! Who would want a son? You seemed flabbergasted at the thought, and from that day forward you expressed sympathy for those who had boys. When you left the hospital you went straight to see George and Angela, waking them up at six in the morning to announce Alison's birth.

He danced all over the apartment, Angela told me later. *Really danced! Jumped up in the air and twirled around! It was something to see!*

In the months that followed, I concentrated on tending our baby, typing your term papers and preparing the many letters of application for teaching jobs at colleges around the country. We agreed that when you'd finished your thesis we'd have another child. When you were offered a job at Malaspina College in Nanaimo, contingent upon your completing your thesis, I thought we were on our way towards a new kind of life, a rounded family life that would unfold in all the predictable ways. Before we married I hadn't intended to become conventional, but now it seemed the inescapable next step.

With the move, our life became more challenging. Our three Montreal apartments had been on streets with elegant names—Claremont, Ste. Famille, Sherbrooke—and our surroundings felt magical. When we moved to Nanaimo, the names of our streets and neighbourhoods took on a new significance; I can see that now as I look back. The first street in our new town was Newton. Then we moved to Lantzville, the weapons were out and we were arguing a lot because you wouldn't finish your thesis. Then there was Two Coves, south of town, and we seemed to be taking two separate directions. I was working part time and taking correspondence courses while you were teaching and fishing and getting involved in local theatre. Not working on your thesis. When I nagged you about it, you explained that you didn't think it was important. You'd spent many years as an undergraduate, getting a good education you assured me, but without completing the language requirements. In the end they changed the requirements and you got the Bachelor's degree retroactively without doing extra work. I think you expected something like that to happen also with the Master's degree, but it didn't.

The early years in Nanaimo were difficult, but things got better when we bought an old house on Park Avenue, where we parked for a few years, and then, taking out a large mortgage, we bought our main family home on a street appropriately named Millstone. But in the end, the time ran out on the Sir George degree requirements. The administration at Malaspina College made it clear that you were required to have an M.A. For a while I thought you might lose your job, but eventually you worked out an arrangement to go for a partial leave so that you could undertake a whole new Master's degree at Simon Fraser University. Again I typed papers for you, but this time I was disagreeable about it. I was relieved that you were holding on to your job but, with a young daughter to care for, I began to worry about the future.

You would only apply yourself to things that interested you and you'd become bored with your graduate work. You just wanted to teach and do whatever else caught your immediate attention: organizing street theatre, writing letters and rants, acting in plays, cooking exotic meals. *We need a long-term plan,* I said to you. More than once. You would look at me and respond with vehemence, *I will never plan. Never! Never!*

Eventually, I learned to accept that you didn't share my concerns, and so I decided to make my plans for myself. I completed a Bachelor's degree at night while working half-time and went on to complete an M.A. in English myself, typing my papers and my own lengthy thesis. Why, I wondered, had it been such a big deal for you to settle down and do the little bit of work that remained to complete your thesis?

For the next few years there were frequent arguments, betrayals, disappointments and disenchantments, but I don't want to write about that. Throughout it all, I admired your vigour and your passion. When things made you angry, you leapt up and waved your arms about, made fearful faces and roared with rage. And then forgot about it. You said I was too concerned with what others thought and that I held myself back too much. *It would do you good to raise your arms, shout, and flail a bit,* you said when I complained. Your enthusiasms were equally expansive, whereas I was often faint-hearted. You need to live harder, you said, and quoted Edgar Le Masters' "Lucinda Matlock": *Degenerate sons and daughters, Life is too strong for you—It takes life to love Life.*

We had a busy household with friends and nephews and nieces coming to stay, lots of dinner parties and big Christmas gatherings with the extended family. You were at your best at Christmas. You could be churlish about the cost of it all, denouncing the extravagance and foolishness of gift-giving, but at a certain point each Christmas Eve, after everything was done—the tree festooned, the presents under it, the kitchen prepped for Christmas morning, Christmas dinner, snacks, etc.—you'd dart off for your last shopping trip to purchase the additional and unnecessary bottle of champagne, the extra couple of presents, the overindulgent box of chocolates, and return laden and beaming. On Christmas morning you donned the devil suit, your long, red, one-piece underwear, and became the Christmas elf.

You led me in a song and dance, I would say, but I think what I loved best in fact was the singing and dancing, which you shared in the classroom as well as at home. Once, in the kitchen, you showed me how you'd given your students a demonstration of ballet, swooping around with your long arms raised above your head and humming an off-key version of "The Dance of the Flowers." *An imitation of the waltz,* you said. You circled ferociously around our kitchen, shouting *Oom pah pah, oom pah, pah...*

That's actually a waltz, I observed.

I can't dance, you insisted. *That was just an imitation.*

You knew a lot about music and, listening to the radio, could often identify not only the work but also which singers were performing, which pianists. You had a good ear, yet were unable to carry a tune. I was sure you could learn and offered to teach you, but you were adamant that you could not, although often you'd suddenly start a kind of tap dance and sing, *I'mmmmmm... puttin' on my top hat... tyin' up my white tie... brushin' off my tails,* with gestures to suggest various props. If it was an imitation of a tap dance, it was a pretty good one.

People spoke of you having *gusto* and *pizzazz.* You added life to our lives. Everything you did was intense and absorbed you completely, whether it was fishing, writing, acting, running marathons. When we swam together, you raced ahead into the water, shouting, *Cowabunga, boys and girls, cowabunga,* then shrieked with the cold. I would tell you to calm down. Too rash, I would say, too ill-advised.

When Alison left to go to university we were lonely and the house felt too large for us. We decided, impulsively, to move to a small house on Brechin Road. The traffic on that road drove us crazy, and when the cars poured off the Departure Bay ferry you would run out to the road and shout, *Go home, peckerheads, go home!* I said, *I guess it was a bad idea to move here,* but you said, *Oh, it's not that. I just want the peckerheads to go home.* A German friend told us that in his language the word *brechin* meant vomit, but I don't know if that's true. Maybe it just meant break-in away from our sadly empty nest.

I invent all these metaphors, mindlessly entertaining myself by trying to make sense of our life together, to give it a shape and a story when it was all quite arbitrary. And yet, our next move to Protection Island was just that. *Protection.* Being on the edge of the ocean in a community of artists, scientists, gardeners, musicians, labourers and layabouts was good for us. Together we had twenty-one years there, reading and writing, travelling and entertaining, cooking and swimming, working and napping, being idle and being happy. I felt that all the jagged pieces of our life had at last come together in a good way, though at the back of our minds we must have known it couldn't last. Now I think back on the island as a kind of Brigadoon, a place that exists through the mists in some other dimension, a place to which I can never return.

It was during those island years that you created your fetish, Mr. Koko, collecting all the scaly worm shells and white oyster shells and spreading them out on the kitchen table. *Don't touch them*, you said, *they are for my fetish.* Neighbours brought over wolf teeth and clam opercula. You gouged out holes for the eyes in the log and attached silvery, bleached driftwood to create spidery arms. After you bound your fetish with hemp rope you glued in blue chiton shells to make eyes. You called him Mr. Koko because you said *Ko Ko* was what the Congolese said when they entered your hut. We had a wonderful celebration on the beach when Mr. Koko was completed, and you placed him by the door of our home.

A fetish symbolizes the co-existence of the spirit world and the physical, a mediator between these worlds, you said. *He will guard us.*

Mr. Koko stared fiercely at the wind and rain, but he couldn't prevent all the inevitable health predicaments. After you'd completed eight marathons, you had problems with your knees that forced you to give up running. That was one of the few times I'd seen you weep. There was breast cancer for me, but we got through that pretty easily. Two small surgeries and a bit of radiation. You had problems with an enlarged prostate but preferred complaining about the number of times you had to pee each day to exploring treatments for it. I had arthritis in both knees, but not so severe that surgery was needed.

We'd sorted out how to live together. You were happy to take on all the physical stuff, running back and forth to town for groceries while I looked after financial arrangements and travel plans. You called yourself *Trotty* after the old man in Dickens' story *The Chimes.* In fact, you were quite a bit like that Trotty, a man who was described as going uncomplainingly about his errands, always cheerful, looking on the bright side. Together we claimed we made up a whole person, me the head and you the body. Neither of us would manage alone. Often I said it was unfortunate that we were so yoked together because we were essentially incompatible.

I don't think we're so incompatible, you said, in the month before you died.

Well, we are, I replied. I wish I'd answered differently. But it was my habit to talk about our dissimilarities, about your love of meat versus my vegetarian leanings, your wish to have the radio on versus my wish for silence, your preference for sweet and mine for savory, your insistence on shutting out the morning light and mine on having the curtains open. *We are opposite in everything,* I would insist, although in truth we were of one mind on so many things.

You were generally a good-natured man, while I was often cross and ill-tempered. At such times you would just pat my head and say, *Cheer up, Kettle, everything will be all right.*

You were exuberant on our travels, making

lively scenes at train stations and airports. Alison talks about the time when I left my big blue straw hat in an airport restaurant and you raced back to get it for me, returning with it on your head as you skipped and danced between our fellow travellers. Once we travelled by train from Toronto to Halifax, and at the end of the day you clambered up to the top berth. I heard you laughing through the night as the train hurtled through the Gaspé and then saw your bare legs descending uncertainly as you announced, *I could bolt out of here in my underwear, but those monkeys, the attendants, would just stuff me back in here, wouldn't they?* As always, I kept a journal of our travels. You decided to write a ditty in it every day. The first one was:

> *When in silks my Carol sails*
> *Along our rusty Eastern rails*
> *Despite the horror in the night*
> *She never shouts out in a fright*
> *And never cries, "Oh, what avails?"*

On our final morning you wrote:

> *When whizzing ballets in the night*
> *Destroy my sleep and give me fright*
> *I think of Carol's shelt'ring love*
> *I find my Goddess from Above*
> *Can armour me with sturdy love.*

Ten days of ditties.

At the end of our vacation, I made a list of its highlights, which numbered 32 events. Why didn't I list the greatest highlight, which was travelling with you, being with you, night and day?

You wrote a piece about that trip and the virtues and vices of train travel called "Hurtle to the Sea." You wrote another piece about trips to Europe called "The Awkward Squad Abroad," in which you spoke of your discomfort with foreign languages and described trying to buy scotch tape in Paris and miming a Highland fling. *It's ruban adhesif,* Alison explained when you complained about the shopkeeper's failure to respond to your performance. And there was the time in Italy when you bought some calzone and insisted that you wanted it *caldo, caldo, par le treno,* then kept snatching it back when the baker tried to heat it for you. How you guffawed when you later realized you'd meant to say *freddo*. You reveled in these pecadillos and repeated those stories happily. We had wonderful trips to Italy, visiting vineyards, writing about wine and food. North to Valdobiaddene for prosecco and grappa, south to Puglia for the rich, red primitivos. You were the best travelling companion.

Years ago, with George and Angela, we played a party game in which we decided who among us had the qualities of charm, charisma, clout or style. George said that you had something better than any of those things: grace. I questioned that, thinking about your excessive behaviors, yet it was true. After all our years together you had a lovely, old-fashioned kind of chivalry. *May I assist you?* you'd ask, if I was struggling with a heavy bag, or *Allow me,* simply hold out a hand, giving a formal bow.

Oh, to be honest, you could also be rude and surprisingly crude at times. You blurted out inappropriate things and you were often thoughtless. But such times were less frequent.

I never knew my life would be so good, you said to a friend, a few months before you died. *I have a smart wife, a wonderful daughter, an exceptional grandchild, great friends. A house on the water. A handsome and intelligent dog. And I've had work I always loved. I could not have imagined such good fortune.*

You taught English at the college all your working life, and after you retired accepted every offer to teach sessional courses or Elder College programs. You said it was an indulgence to stand at the front of a classroom talking about books all day.

Through the years I've worked off and on at many different jobs, often part-time, while you stuck with teaching. I was the octopus, you were the barnacle. In the end of my working life I became an administrator at the college and you were proud of that, but I always felt sure that your work was more important and more honourable.

I would sometimes boast, *Who knows what I might have done had I not been yoked to you and marooned in this small town? Whereas you would still be in a room in Kitsilano making duck soup if it weren't for marrying me.*

Occasionally you'd point out that I'd been an anxious high school dropout when you met me, that it was only your teachings that gave me the confidence to better myself. That was certainly true, but the last time I told you how lucky you were, you said, seriously, *You are right. I was lucky to acquire such a wife. I got her at a weak moment.*

When were you not part of me? This is what I can never recall. Even now, I still experience life as "we" and not "I," our home and possessions as "ours" and not "mine." Did I see that play alone or with you? Weren't you with me when I bought those new towels? Didn't you hear that recording of "The Great Gazzoon"? Did you ever see Charlotte in her school uniform? Of course not! But when did it all change? When did I become just me? I can't remember, can't distinguish.

Eventually, I'll sort some of this out—which was you, which me, when were we together, when was I alone. Of course, I know that you weren't here through last spring, summer, fall. Obviously, you weren't with me on that last lonely trip to Montreal. But I have to work hard to remind myself that you weren't, because every cell in my body still holds you and counts on you being with me as you were for so many days, weeks, months and years. Nights. Especially nights.

I keep coming back to the recognition that through the days and years and decades of our marriage we often sometimes didn't see each other as individuals. In becoming "we", we often lost the "I" and the "Thou." There were many moments when the lack of differentiation was wonderful— the glance that communicated the thought, the private language, the sense of being one—but I wish I'd seen you as clearly as I do now.

I wish I had paid more attention to you, especially towards the end when I failed to notice what was happening, the cancer spreading through your body and in your brain. I was in shock and experienced it as happening not to you but to us.

We didn't know, you said, when the referral was made to palliative care, *we didn't know.* I feel I should have known, even though your doctor didn't know although we consulted her twice in the month before you went to hospital.

And yet, there were such good days, especially in that last year together, on those late summer and autumn mornings when I awoke and turned to you to say, *Well, then, another day!* When we'd sip a slow coffee together on the deck, planning the day. A morning putter, lunch, reading, a swim, an afternoon nap.

This is the bonus time, I said often. *Our work done, our daughter settled with her family. We're free to do whatever we want.*

These are the times we will remember when we are dead, you replied somberly, *a line from a story you liked.*

It wasn't so long ago, those days when our lives were about a rich harvest. Now, in the winter of my life, the view is bleak. Stark. Looking from my bedroom window I can see the shape of the trees, the leaves having fallen. I see the stark sky.

In the very end, we are all left with only the "I." My task now is to know that person whom I've become, the person I am becoming, yet I find myself still yearning for those days of belonging, for the many thousands of mornings when we awoke together with a sense of having day after day ahead. I see us as we were at first, walking up the hill from the Atwater Market, loaded down with green tomatoes, red apples, ripe cheeses and spicy sausages, and sometimes a big purple eggplant, and spreading our harvest out over the little table in our tiny Claremont kitchen. *Exalted manna, gladness of the best...* I see us in that spring before Alison was born, after we'd sold my piano to make way for her crib and were decorating her room, imagining how our lives would change. *Heaven in ordinary... something understood.*

There were seasons after seasons of belonging, of being connected, of our small family travelling together. The memory that stays with me is of a day when the three of us took a little float plane to a remote spot on Sonora Island where we were looking at a property of which we might lease a share. Awaiting the plane's return a few hours later, we walked the deserted shore at low tide and decided to see if we could enact the pattern of the solar system as we'd read about in Norman Malcolm's memoir of Wittgenstein. I was the sun, walking slowly along the beach, you were the planet earth, running counterclockwise circles around me, and we assigned Alison the most difficult role of the moon, racing around you as you circled around me.

It was exhausting, exhilarating and unforgettable, like our years together. The image that remains with me is of three separate entities in a vast, shared universe, endlessly and exquisitely linked in time and space.

Give sorrow words, the grief that does not speak knits up the o-er wrought heart and bids it break.

Macbeth, *William Shakespeare*

Mourning

April 1, 2012. I am getting ready to speak at your memorial service. As on the day we were married, I have had to tranquillize myself. An Ativan to face the day when I first awoke and another to prepare myself for the event. The date was chosen not just because of your love of foolishness, but also because you claimed it was the birthday of our dog, Victor.

In the days after your death, I anguish over plans, wanting to honour you in the best way possible. A small group of friends meet with Alison and me to help us sort out where and how the memorial should be held. We choose an auditorium in a nearby park, an open space with lots of windows looking out to the trees, and we spend hours and days talking about music, speakers and food.

Our musician friends from the island, Rick

Scott, David Essig and Jenny Cluff play at the start and end of the service, and a sound system is set up to play the *Kyrie Eleison* and the *Lacrimosa* of Mozart's *Requiem*. You'd said you wanted the *Requiem* at your funeral, but we can't do the full hour so we settle for just two selections.

A nephew, a niece, a friend, a colleague, and Alison and I speak in the program, which is introduced by two old friends who wear your favourite hats and speak eloquently about you. The caterer has prepared elegant little servings of finger food on tables covered with flowers and pottery wheelbarrows filled with vegetables to acknowledge your love of the community garden. The women in my writing group don white aprons and serve large platters of appetizers while the mourners stand and talk in small groups. People stay for a long time.

I'm glad we waited until six weeks after you died to hold the memorial. It gave us time to think about what we wanted. I believe it was just as it should have been, and yet too little and too late. I've heard other widows use the same expression. Maybe it takes death to show us the possibility our marriages held.

Earlier, a memorial for you was held on Protection Island. Others planned it without any effort or involvement on my part. It was the kind of island event you'd have loved, with the local musicians playing your favourite songs, songs like *You'll Need Somebody on Your Bond* and *Fly Away*. The community hall was full of flowers and packed with neighbours who'd brought assorted chilis and various kinds of pie in recognition of your passion for and prowess at creating these dishes. Someone remembered how happy you were when the Saskatoon berries turned up in the grocery store, and so she made one of those pies. There was such a feeling of love in the room.

But that event was so soon after your death that Alison and I were both really raw. Somehow we managed to speak. She read a few lines of one of your poems. I talked about whatever came into my mind, telling stories about your medical theories, trying to make people laugh. I sniffled throughout, but I got through it.

The tributes began even earlier, in the days before you were moved to palliative care. When you were first in hospital, we started a blog as a way of distributing updates to let friends and family know how your treatment was progressing and when you would be back home. We called it "Surviving and Prevailing." When it was clear that your situation was critical, friends began to respond with stories and photographs of happy times with you.

A nephew wrote about a favourite memory

from when he was 10 years old and with you in the shopping mall:

> Mike pulled a purple rubber octopus from his pocket and as we wandered through the mall he tossed it onto shop windows and watched with glee. At one point he picked a particularly tall window on the other side of two very serious men wearing serious suits in a serious office having what appeared to be a very serious discussion. As the little toy reached the bottom of their office window, they were smiling and laughing. I remember thinking at the time that the world would be a much better place if more grown-ups were like my Uncle Mike." In hindsight, it was an epiphany.

A 10-year-old great-nephew wrote:

> I remember the time when Mike gave me a rubber fried egg and I tried to cut it and eat it. This reminds me that Mike is always handy for a practical joke. No matter what it is, he always makes me laugh (a lot). Keep the fight going!

A friend of Alison's wrote that she remembered:

> Mike at Christmas time, singing the "bring me flesh and bring me wine" line in Good King Wenceslas with great force and theatricality

(can't you just hear it!?); Mike wrangling floppy disks, and all their inherent problems, long after they faded from the computing scene. There is this pure sparkle and originality and joie de vivre in Mike's encounters with life, good stuff and bad. Mike is just so damn good at life.

A former student wrote about being in your class and said:

I think it must have looked like I was hanging on his every word, but in truth I sometimes faded off into a fit of fondness for his enthusiasm, his thoughtful looks directed at the ceiling and his boundless positivity. So while he was saying something clever, I was basking in his energy and thinking, "Mike Matthews, I just love you to bits."

The blog took on a life of its own, which made everything more ominous, but I was glad to be able to read some of the messages aloud to you. It was the beginning of the acknowledgement. Words, words. Speaking the grief.

The day after the island memorial, the water heater exploded. *That's funny,* someone said. *The same thing happened when Annie's husband died last year.* Of course, it was anything but funny. On a cold March morning, with grief-stricken family in every bedroom, you need hot water. It was as though there were tears coming from the house as well as from the skies. Rose-Lynn Fisher, a photographer, has created a project called *The Topography of Tears* in which she shows magnified microscopic images of tears of laughter, tears of relief, tears of possibility and tears of grief. They're all beautiful but, to me, the photograph of the tears of grief is much emptier than the others.

The news of my damaged water heater spread quickly, and in a matter of hours a neighbour called. He'd ordered a new water heater to be delivered in four days. He arranged its installation and saw to the removal of the old one. Neither he nor the young men who handled the transport would take any money for anything.

It helped. Nothing lessens the loss, but the kindness of others softens the edges.

For ten years, we'd had a small apartment on Harwood Street in the West End of Vancouver as well as our island home. Later we sold it and bought a townhouse in Nanaimo, a place from which we could do some work and also escape winter weather. The Nanaimo townhouse was a blessing when we had medical appointments, when you first were ill and then in hospital. But we continued to spend most of our time on Protection Island, which was, for us, a real sanctuary, being very close to Vancouver Island yet so far from the commercial concerns of the city.

It's still a sanctuary, but a bleak place without you. The tides, higher again this year, have been rising almost to the rosemary plants on the shoreline. I can see that some of the logs you pushed up against the bank have started to roll out to sea. The big log on the point is still there, but with every high tide, it rocks back and forth precipitously. For how long, I wonder now?

We might have torn down the original cabin and built a new house further from the shore, but we liked the little cottage, so we built an addition onto the old structure. We liked the drama of the winter storms We liked walking out the front door right to the beach on hot summer days. We could almost dive from our deck into the ocean. It felt like the edge of the world, in the best possible way.

Some people are plucky during the time of mourning, but I am crabby. I whinge a lot. Some of the plucky ones believe that life is an event in which the goal is to overcome obstacles, perform well and, if possible, win the race. A man told a friend whose wife had suddenly died that the thing was to get right back up on that horse again. What horse? Now I know that every response to death and mourning is unique.

There's a cynical dictum that claims that women grieve and men replace. Of course, this is a generalization and I don't think it's that simple, but women do seem to remain bereaved for a longer period. They continue to mourn.

We all have our own ways of viewing our marriages. There are those who see themselves as a central character in a movie and imagine their lives as visually appealing and superficially significant. *I just wanted her to meet me at the door wearing an apron, a little dab of flour on her nose,* one man told me as he mourned for the loss of his wife who had run off with another man. *We never did romantic things like walking through the woods, kicking at the fall leaves,* a woman friend complained to me when her husband left. *You know, just kicking at the fall leaves.*

Others see life as a complex narrative, a novel with twists and turns, with surprising events that can derail everything forever. They perceive small losses as irreplaceable and significant. A box of Christmas decorations is accidentally dropped and the small, red china clock, in your family for decades, crumbles into smithereens. The familiar corner store, which always carried your Sunday paper, burns down. Your old cat disappears, never to be seen again. Such events are deeply felt, studied and must be interpreted as part of a life story. This way of dealing with loss is often very difficult and it takes time. It's not easy to behave well when you are immersed in such memories. I admire those who are resilient, but I tend to weep and mourn.

Some people view life as a marathon, and so they press onwards, steadily and directly, right through to the finish line. Others see it as a pilgrimage, with many pauses for reflection, regret, expiation and celebration, and many set-backs and backward steps along the way. And yet some pilgrims are also grimly fixated on the goal and careful to avoid distractions. It is impossible to make judgments about how people deal with grief, but well-meaning friends often urge the bereaved to "move on," when in fact they cannot heal their grief except through extended mourning, which is troubling for friends and family.

Trubba not, Nanna, nine-year-old Charlotte says, patting my shoulder when she finds me, a few days after your death, alone and in tears in our bed-room. *We'll swim this lake,* she says. A year ago, a school assignment required her to interview an older person about a challenge they had faced and overcome, I told her that, as a child her age, I'd wanted to swim across Kakawa Lake, where my family spent summer holidays. At first my parents refused to let me attempt it but, after I'd nagged them for the whole year, they reluctantly agreed. My father and brother accompanied me in a row-boat, assured by my promise to climb in as soon as I tired. It was arduous and a couple of times I paused to tread water or float on my back for a bit, but I was determined. And, to everyone's surprise, I swam to the other side.

So you see, I'd told Charlotte, *if you set your mind to it, you can do things that others think to be impossible.*

And now she comforts me with my own history. She already understands metaphor, I realize, amazed that the story has stayed with her and that she had some awareness of mourning. And when she'd said "we," she had included herself in the challenge. *We'll swim this lake.*

It is such a "journey," as they say these days. There are no words for the pain of it. Julian Barnes, in his book *Levels of Life* says that grief is vertical and mourning is horizontal. I tell Alison, *At times I can get above the grief, but I can never get beyond the mourning. It goes on forever.* A recently widowed friend liked the Barnes quotation but for her it meant something different: that grief is solitary but mourning is shared, part of a broader space, which I think is more comforting to her.

According to my mother, the funeral procession for my great-grandfather on Mile End Road in East London over a hundred years ago was an impressive affair. Although the family was destitute as a result of his drinking and gambling, my great-grandmother scraped and borrowed enough money to hire six black horses decked out with black ostrich feathers to convey his coffin to the graveyard in an elegant carriage. As a child, I was transfixed. How splendid those horses must have looked!

It was ridiculous, my mother said. *The family was so poor that your grandmother had to leave school and work as a seamstress when she was just a little child. It was a foolish display for a drunkard who neglected his family.*

So why did she do it?

To honour him. She was in deep mourning for two years. Dressed in black crepe, wearing a long veil. Ridiculous!

That's what the mourning period was once about: the public display of inner grief. In Victorian days, men had black gloves, hatbands and cravats while women wore black silk dresses, trimmed with black crepe but without lace or jewelry. For the period of full or "deep" mourning, one or two years for a widow, they wore black veils and bonnets when they left the house, and only later, in "half-mourning," wore grey or mauve. Everyone recognized these symbols and behaved appropriately. Nowadays it's not clear how to publicly acknowledge our losses. Neither the widow nor her friends are quite sure how to behave.

For a while our life together was paradise. Now, on the other side of paradise, I wait for the ocean to engulf me, to sweep our little home out to sea, a frail little ark. It becomes harder and harder to spend time on the island. You loved all versions of the Noah story, didn't you? P.K. Page's *Cry Ararat*; that strange little story by Jacques Ferron; *The Flood*; Robert Duncan's, *The Ballad of Mrs. Noah*. Well, what I'd like to ask you right now is this: what about when the flood overtakes the ark and the old woman is left alone, while all the others have paired off elsewhere? When Mrs. Noah is a timeworn widow. The story is still evolving for me.

It is clear to me that mourning doesn't end with the immediate public response of honouring; the internal mourning period is ongoing. Being alone in the world while enduring the loss. It's endless. Every time I come home I hear your voice exclaiming, *It's you!* or *You're here! You're here!* Every time I leave, I cry a little, and I turn the radio on when I go out just so that it won't be so damn silent when I return and open the door to our empty house.

I keep imagining you bursting through the door, shouting, *Hello, this place!* I miss having your response to all the things that are happening these days. What would you say about this year's tax assessment? About the tartan kilt Charlotte must wear to her new school? About her move to that new school? Her continued refusal to eat food that is not utterly bland? I can imagine you saying lots of things, and I know just how you would respond to Charlotte's great success at getting those basketballs into the hoop, but I don't know exactly which peculiar words you would use, what jokes you'd make. Your responses were always a surprise. I can project from what you used to say, but what would you say about the things you never knew? What would you say about the proposed development of our lovely working harbour with its mixed usage, fishing boats, rowboats, sailboats, passenger ferry? The plan to turn it into a parking lot for large visiting yachts? I make a mental list of the words you might use—*maggots, numskulls, turkeyburgers, dunderheads, troglodytes*—but there's nothing new, nothing surprising coming from you now and there always, always, was before.

New ideas, new words. The names you had for people you didn't know. *Horse Thief,* for the silent man who lived down the road. *Angel Woman* and *Jazz Man*, an attractive couple we thought we'd like to get to know. *The Vulgarsons*, for a less appealing couple.

Without you, there's less for me to talk about. So much of my conversation with others was made up of, *And you know what Mike said about that?* I got a lot of mileage out of your responses. I was always quoting you. Now that I'm alone, I must find my own words.

A couple of widows have told me that they have no regrets. How can that be? What would that feel like? Were there no senseless arguments? Did they never do or say unforgiveable things? I have a thousand regrets and I go over them again and again, working back from my failure to go to bed at the same time as you on that last night, through to my crabbiness during our last few weeks when I was so stressed and anxious, and further back to my failure to go to every one of your races and marathons and my disinclination to go fishing with you. Not that you ever seemed really keen to have me there for those things, and, of course, there were lots of occasions on which you chose not to accompany me.

But in fact, we did most things together, could never have imagined planning separate holidays. I went away alone on a couple of occasions, only because you couldn't or wouldn't take time off work, and even then we emailed or talked on the phone every day. We frequently acknowledged our good fortune in being with the only person in the world who we never found boring or tedious. Yet I find myself thinking about how much I took you for granted. I think I will pay for that. *The mills of God grind slowly, yet they grind exceeding fine.*

I continue to be filled with regret about my crabbiness. About my failure to save your life, to defeat the crab. I've heard that in some places people tear the large claw off crabs because they contain the most meat, an especially sweet meat that is considered a delicacy, and then chuck the amputated crab back in the ocean with the thought that it will grow another claw. Many of them carry on and regenerate enough that they become fit for another capture, another amputation.

On our wedding night, you devoured Crab Newburg in a fancy New England restaurant, whereas I would never eat crab, not wanting any part of it. Not the catching, the cracking, the cooking, nor the consuming. I don't even like the regeneration possibility. I would be one of those crabs who crawled away and died.

You didn't crawl, though, did you? You raced.

Remember those days when nobody we knew had cancer? Before I had breast cancer, before the crab crept into your body, when we joked about the notion of "battling" cancer? You said yours would be a cowardly defeat, not a brave battle. *All right*, you would say, *you win.*

I wouldn't have embarked on warfare for my own life, either, but now I wish I had fought harder for your life until the last possible second. Raged at the doctors, resisted palliative care. Insisted on seeing the oncologist, whatever the doctor said. Never mind how much pain you might have been in. I wish I could have kept you with me at any price and in any state.

Maybe, like the crab, you could have regenerated, revived enough to receive treatment. Treatment after treatment after treatment, waiting patiently for the next amputation. For the resurrection. You had never been in hospital until this happened and you hated the thought of being an invalid, but you did appreciate Wendell Berry's words about putting your faith in the two inches of humus that will build under the trees. *Practice resurrection,* he said.

I can't practice resurrection but I'm going to try to practice a *gedankenexperiment,* which is the term for a thought experiment, one that is carried out in the imagination only. I'm experimenting right now by having you come up behind me and place your hands on my shoulders while I sit at the computer, draping your jacket over me because I've complained of cold. I hold it around me, listening to your footsteps as you walk away.

Everywhere I find evidence of your presence: notes scribbled on odd bits of paper, old letters, messages tucked in books. Whenever I'm at the computer I rediscover photographs and emails from you: *It is nice to have so many ways of quickly getting hold of one's beloved,* says one email, *but that doesn't stop the pangs of lonely that zing out at me... I will phone you later.*

No more. No more. *Well, then, another day,* I would say in the morning.

Shhh, you'd reply. *Sleepy time now.*

When the battle's done and ended, there'll be time enough for sleep. I'd prod you gently. *Up lad, up, tis late for lying...*

Not yet, not yet.

Awake. Awake, for the sun has scattered stars

before him from the field of night. Who wrote that, anyway?

The Rubaiyat. Omar Khayyam, Hush. Hush.

Another day,

When the battle's done and ended, there'll be time enough for sleep. Who wrote that?

Shhhhhhhhh.

Love you, kiddo.

We felt these days would last forever.

We didn't know. We didn't know, you said, when you were transferred to the palliative care ward. The world changed in an instant, and eight days later you were dead.

Almost every fall we'd go back to Montreal to visit old stomping grounds, old friends. This time I go alone, as a pilgrimage, as a tribute to you, the keeping of a promise. The city welcomes me, as always, and it's comfortable to be in the familiar quarters we shared for so many holidays through the years. John and Audrey are easy and informal, going about their own activities and leaving me to do what I will. On the first morning with them, I get up to find a note from Audrey, who has left me breakfast supplies but is already out of the house. For a moment I'm almost happy, certainly content, as I shower, dress and plan my day. Sitting alone at the dining table with my coffee and notebook, I pick up the earrings you bought me many years ago from a little shop around the corner on Victoria Avenue. I'd admired them and you surprised me by going out later to buy them. It seems right for me to be wearing them today, but as I try to put on the second earring, it slips through my fingers. I try several times before I notice that my pierced ear has split open. There is no pain, no blood, but I do remember feeling a tug at my ear lobe as I turned in the night.

Now I have a cleft ear! I used to accuse you of having a cloven hoof, but a cleft ear is something else. What does it mean? Are you sending me a message? I put the earrings away and go out with my ears bare. I feel naked without them. Later that night, Audrey hunts through an old jewelry chest, which belonged to her mother, and finds two pairs of clip-earrings.

I'm sure you can get that ear fixed, she reassures me.

It must be significant, so I will leave my ear as is, I reply. *Cleft. I wasn't meant to go about my travels without noticing how the world had changed. How I have been changed.*

Montreal is as vital as ever. We used to speak of the electricity in the air, the sheer zing of energy we feel walking the streets. People are alive in this city. They look up and around, and don't just stare down at their feet or gaze off into the distance. As always, I feel the energy around me but I can no longer connect to it.

Tonight I've been thinking about all the cancer in the world. Thinking about one of my former colleagues, a younger man, who died just after you, suddenly, also of undiagnosed lung cancer. Like me, his wife is reeling with the loss but I have no room to comfort others and cannot bear to attend his memorial. Many people we know are facing, fighting or failing to defeat cancer. It is an epidemic. I remember when, years ago in Oxford, on a walk with a friend who pointed out the dead fish in a garden pool, you said, *Someday we will all turn warty and float to the top of the pond.* Now it's happening.

The topic of Cancer is always on my mind. Cancer was first named by Greek physicians, apparently in relation to some tumours that had a crablike appearance. Its etymological root is the Greek *karkinos*, and it means tumour or spreading sore, and also the Zodiac name, which was later used to designate the Cancer constellation. The mythology of Cancer the Crab and its appearance in the spring night sky has to do with one of the Twelve Labours of Hercules, the son of Zeus and his lovely mistress Alcmene, the queen of Tiryns. Zeus's wife, Hera, was angry about Zeus's infidelity and so when Hercules faced his battle with Hydra, the water serpent, Hera sent a giant crab to distract and destroy him by nipping at his heels. Hercules responded by kicking the crab up to the heavens.

The constellation of Cancer is about 580 light years away from us in a drift of stars. A beehive of stars. Of blue stars in fact.

Blue star, when I am blue, all I do, is dream of you...

Thinking about the crab reminds me of how I go up or down stairs crab-style these days. My bad knees have made me crabby over the past few years. I'm outwardly more cheerful than I feel, and almost certainly less crabby than I was with you. You let me be crabby and said I had good reason for it. You allowed me to be who I was: a crab. *It is my nature,* I told you, reminding you of the story about the scorpion and the tortoise. The tortoise generously agrees to carry the scorpion across the river, but halfway across the scorpion stings him and the tortoise sinks. When asked why he has done this thing that will cause them both to die, the scorpion replies, *It's my nature.*

Nature. Consciousness. Sentience. Those are the big questions. Sometimes, sitting at the ocean's edge, I imagine the enormous variety of creatures crawling about on the ocean floor, the invisible cellular life in the water itself. I think about the tiny limpets returning again and again to the same spot after daily excursions around the rocky shores. They have an awareness of what home is. An enormous collection of microorganisms live on my skin or in my body. Bacteria and fungi reside in my saliva or my gastrointestinal tract. Do they too have a sense of home, of me as their host?

I know that dogs feel deeply. Victor, though stoic about pain, as you were, still mourns your death. He is a sentient being, and generally seems more aware than I am. He mourns. Even now he sniffs at your clothes closet and wears a mournful expression. I'm not imagining this. I've read that grief is one of the basic emotions dogs feel. When they mourn they usually sleep more than normal, move slower, eat less and don't play as much, all true of Victor these days. There are many heart-breaking stories of dogs waiting for their masters' return, sometimes for years after the owner's death. Dogs are capable of a deep devotion.

My friend Rachel sent me this little verse she claimed was dictated by Victor:

Bark 1

His Hand, His Scent, His Voice
Not there.
He ran. A ball
Thrown out of sight.

Bark 2

Her Eyes, Her Hand, Her Voice
Still here.

She sees me sad
And holds me tight.

Bark 3

Tears on my fur.
My job is now
To make Her glad.
And We're all right.

Yes, we are both all right, but we feel your absence.

I know Mike will be with you, a friend says about our forthcoming wedding anniversary. I felt Mike's presence, says another, about a gathering a friend held for me. *How do they know such things?* How can it be that they are able to feel your presence when I do not? *He will be sitting on your shoulder,* says one dear friend. It gives me pause, that comment. You were not a small man. But I know what they mean, and I know they mean well. They believe your spirit is still here and they say such things to give me comfort.

Well. Well. Will all manner of things be well? *You're doing really well,* people say to me now. But what do they mean? What do they know? What is it that they see? Not what's inside of me.

It's hard being around other couples. Those who are always snuggling up to each other, or worse, the ones, not young, who fondle each other, stroking and kissing. It feels cruel, insensitive, maybe even hostile, but it is probably just thoughtless and a bit narcissistic. I can't help but think of Oscar Wilde's observation that flirting in married couples is disgusting, *washing their clean linen in public*. Do they want me to leave? Some carp and bicker, as we often used to do, and I'd like to warn them that they will not always have each other, that they should cherish this time. The couples I most like to be with are the ones who do neither of these things, yet between whom I can feel a current of connection, the intimacy that comes from years of compatibility. Fortunately, I see quite a few of those.

Sometimes, I'm plunged into such sorrow that I seriously consider suicide. Then, I recall how you always made me laugh. I remember your medical theories, in which you would explain the ways in which doctors tried to bamboozle the public into thinking very simple things were complicated.

Consider the circulatory system, you would say. *How can anyone believe that business of the red and blue tubes carrying the blood back and forth to the heart? If you prick yourself anywhere, do you not bleed? You can't always be hitting one of those tubes! There's blood everywhere, no system to it at all. It just seeps all over.*

You had an explanation for every medical matter, and made these pronouncements with great solemnity.

And, as to pregnancy and the romance of the brave sperm swimming up the fallopian tubes and magically meeting a ripening egg? No! The truth is, women often don't look after themselves, they get lazy, they leave dishes in the sink, and a little infection sets in. Before you know it, there's a baby!

Remembering, I laugh out loud and feel a surge of love for you, for life, for the world. For something greater than the two of us.

In those last days when I sat beside you, holding your hand and talking about whatever I did, I remembered a spring day a few years earlier when you cut out a Tennessee Williams' poem "Your Blinded Hand" from *The New Yorker* and said it reminded you of us... *in a city of fire when the earth is afire, I must still believe that somehow I would find your blinded hand.* I pasted the poem in my journal, agreeing that, yes, somehow we'd always hear each other's cry, find each other's hand. And during those last days in palliative care, you did very often reach out for my blinded hand, and it was there.

I don't fear death, but I fear the way it will end for me, without you at my side. I sometimes find satisfaction in knowing that you've escaped the grief I feel. Sometimes I imagine myself dead and you alone at the dining table, bent over the crossword puzzle. Or searching for important documents that should be somewhere but aren't. Or in the kitchen, making a solitary supper, dropping things and cursing. Alone, maybe even weeping, reaching out for a blinded hand. For a moment I can be pleased that I am the one who is left alone. This is my last gift to you, suffering the bereavement. It will be different for me at the end.

In the meantime, I still play Solitaire on the computer. And, guess what? I've now reached 47%! And it only took me 23,0512 games to get to this place.

Last night I awoke from a dream in which we were at a market and I lost track of where I was, where you were. I awoke in a fright and called your name aloud twice, before I realized I was alone. It's not surprising that I still expect you to be there beside me at night. In the forty-six-and-a-half years in which we were together there were, at most, twenty days a year when we slept apart, except for the year when I moved to Nanaimo six weeks ahead of you. So if I multiply 46.5 times 345 less 43 that would come to 16,512 days, give or take a few. Compared to the 342 days that I have been without you, that would mean this bereavement phase is only 2% of our time together.

I'm better at Solitaire than I am at being solitary. And there is an unavoidable lesson in Solitaire: sometimes you have a run of good luck and then you just lose and lose, and can't seem to make a comeback.

You taught me so much. I counted on you to tell me who wrote things, what new fashions were about, what dreadful new discoveries were being made in the world, and where. I remember observing that your mind was full of trivia while mine was full of deep thoughts, yet I absolutely depended on you to answer those trivial questions. And, in fact, they weren't trivial at all. They were the important details of life. Now I find that my memories have big gaps without you to fill in the details of the people or the plays, the galleries or the concerts. A young friend wrote that she remembered coming for dinner with us and you mentioning a kind of china called *faience*. She hadn't known the term but said you went off and brought a dictionary back to the table while explaining what it was, referring to luster-ware, a specific kind of china. I don't remember that conversation. If we actually had any *faience* china, I would not have known. You did. She also said of you that the line in Talking Heads' song "This Must be the Place"—out of all those other people, you've got a face with a view—was one she used as a sorter of people. Even when she was young, she knew you had a face with a view.

On our last evening together, the night you were taken to hospital, as we were driving to a restaurant for dinner you said, out of the blue with your voice breaking, *I think, whatever road I must travel in this life, I want to travel it with you.* I reached for your hand and said, *But we do! We will!* After a moment, you added, intense with emotion, *You've given me something which I would never otherwise have had, which I can only describe as "consciousness."* I replied, *You've given me my life. I would be dead without you. I was in bad shape back then.*

I'm glad we had that conversation, but I wish you were here to tell me what exactly you meant by consciousness. I've been reading Walter Sichel's *The Sands of Time*, a lovely assembly of recollections and reflections published in 1923. In it he writes of an experience that a friend of his grandmother had in consulting a clairvoyant, a perfectly ignorant, ordinary woman who fell into a trance and described an unknown place where the woman's son was living and where he was sitting down to write a letter of good cheer to his mother, which, she said, would arrive shortly and, in due course, it did. Sichel, a most rational man, asks,

> *Is it not quite possible that this gift of the far-sight may be one of those primitive senses— like the far-hearing and the far-scent—that civilization has extinguished save in the primitives, who are often among the commonest and the least instructed?*

He goes on to describe experiences of aborigines

getting wind of occurrences hundreds of miles away. It is absurd, says Sichel, to classify a faculty like this as spirit-rapping or planchette. He proposes that there may be a consciousness that allows us to escape the limits of a mere five senses and cross the dimensions of space and time.

Lately I've been re-reading my old journals and in one, several years ago, I find that I've written out these words from St. Julian of Norwich: *Love is not changed by death and nothing is lost, and all in the end is harvest.*

When we were young, we told each other that we were right to spend all our money on whatever places and pleasures interested us, for, we said, *they can take things away from you but they can't take away your memories.* Later, though, I asked you, *What good would our memories be if we didn't have each other to share them?* And you agreed.

For the last few years I have felt your absence keenly and painfully, yet now my memories and our journals provide a kind of harvest and a sense that our love is not lost. As Paolo Coelho says, *Love always triumphs over what we call death. That's why there's no need to grieve for our loved ones, because they continue to be loved and remain by our side.*

here is the deepest secret nobody knows
(here is the root of the root and the bud of the bud
and the sky of the sky of a tree called life; which
grows
higher than soul can hope or mind can hide)
and this is the wonder that's keeping the stars apart
i carry your heart (i carry it in my heart)

I Carry Your Heart, *e.e.cummings*

Cleaving

February 25, 2014. I can feel that things are beginning to change for me. Two years have passed, and though I'm still gathering up the pieces, I'm starting to have a better understanding of where and who I am without you. The hardest thing is having to let go. I keep your notebooks, your pens, most of your many pairs of glasses, your shirts, your shoes. Shirts and shoes. Those were the topics of two stories you wrote in the last few years: *Shoe Time* and *Getting Shirty.* You always did tend towards animism, reluctant to discard any object that had once been important to you and were moved by the thought of some small thing that may have been left out in the rain.

I even keep some of the old shopping lists I find tucked in your jacket pockets. And scraps of papers in desk drawers. *Not enough temptation to fetch Christ, let alone bring Satan to your door*, says one.

Another says, T*he word 'multiple' is exploding. It's all over the place. Maybe I never noticed it before. What's wrong with 'many'?*

Periodically, I've tried to scale down our possessions. I used to accuse you of sentimentality as we argued about what could be recycled. *But not that nice old coffee mug,* you'd say. *Not the map of Puglia. Not the old LPs,* though we no longer had a turntable. Now I cling to those sentimental things.

But, as I gather together these vestiges of you, I realize that I've reached a kind of turning point. I pull on my cleft ear and reflect that the word cleave can mean two things: to cling, to adhere or to split, to separate. Although I've been split apart from you, I still cling to you, cling to shreds of memories. Our marriage now is spliced through and spliced together. Bereft and grieving, yet cleft and cleaving.

It was important for me to gather together a collection of your stories, poems, reviews and rants and publish them under the title *My Faculties at Large,* just as it was necessary to fix up our home before selling it. Our nephew cleaned out the shed that you were always promising you would have organized one day. Years ago, you played Aston in Pinter's *The Caretaker,* a character who hoards useless objects and envisions his shed as the solution to all his difficulties. *You really are Aston,* I'd say. *It was a good performance, but really it was just type casting.* And indeed Aston had a sweet nature and he was a true caretaker, so it was a natural role for you.

You'd be pleased to see how neat and orderly the shed is now. When I sold the house it was in better order than it had ever been during our twenty-two years there together. It felt like a necessary part of the mourning process. Like the laying out, washing and dressing the body. *Oh, dear Mike, how I wish I'd done that myself, and not left it to the nurses and the undertaker.* I was in such shock. I didn't know what I was doing. What I was not doing.

I've moved some distance along the horizontal path of mourning, but often a vertical shaft of grief strikes me like lightning and I can hardly keep from howling. You were such a large and solid presence, so substantial, so constant. It's still unthinkable that you are absent.

Among your many papers is an enormous accordion file, its contents collected over decades. I periodically discarded letters, cards, papers and newspaper clippings from my desk, but you kept everything and your file captures fragments of all our years together. I try to piece them together now, and wish I could ask you questions. *Who sent you the postcard from Turkey? How did you come by the program from the Kerrisdale Presbyterian Church listing me as a soloist? Why did the father of the girl you first loved write to you so frequently, when there's only one letter from the girl herself?*

And the big question: *where have you gone?* You're not any place I can imagine, yet sometimes I sense that you are everywhere. It's a paradox. Tibetan Buddhist meditation master Mingyur Rinpoche made good use of paradoxes—especially hard ones like, *You need to try to master the ability to feel sad without actually being sad.* I almost understand what that means, yet I can't do it.

When our daughter was born you spoke of the miracle it was that a hospital room that held only me, the doctor and the nurse suddenly contained four! It's the same way with death: at one moment there was Alison, you, me and Victor, and an instant later there were only two people with a dog. And mostly just one person. Me.

But sometimes, when I'm cold, I feel you wrapping a sweater or jacket around my shoulders. On winter evenings, I imagine you lighting a fire in the old woodstove. On dark mornings, I see you flinging back the curtains and letting the light in. When the sun bursts through the clouds on a dull day I find myself thinking of Michael, the archangel, *Sword of God. Michaelangelo,* I say to myself. *My angel.*

A friend sent me a eulogy written by author and journalist Aaron Freeman, who proposed that grieving families needed a physicist to remind them that no energy is created in the universe and none is destroyed, that every particle of who we are and have been remains in our world. It's reassuring to think that nothing of you has disappeared, that all your energy is still around but just less orderly. As a friend said, *Mike was always a bit less orderly than most of us, but now he's even more disorderly.*

Bereavement may not be the truncation of a marriage, but it is a truncation of the person left behind. I am abridged, having lost half the person I knew myself to be. More than my ear has been cleft. It's as if someone has taken a cleaver and split me in two, sliced off that part of me that is you. My better half. Even now, two years after your death, I feel as if I am hemorrhaging. Like that iconic old couple Darby and Joan, we were never happy "asunder." *Asunder.* A word that describes bereavement well: we have been broken apart into separate parts, pieces, or places.

I cleave to the certainty that you are here in our daughter, our granddaughter. I see you in their bodies, their smiles. It pleased you that they both have your love of words. When you complained about the dreariness of a song on the radio and Charlotte, aged ten, agreed. *I call that sea urchin music,* she said.

I'm thinking of the colour blue again. It's elusive, incomprehensible, impossible to describe. Years ago at Christmas, P.K. Page sent me a hand-written copy of one of her poems called "Blue."

Tell me how to show
delphinium and lupin
These two summer blues
are blues I cannot send you
in any of my letters

If she couldn't capture the colour blue, how can I?
It is a conundrum, paradoxical, a thing unto itself.
Like grief.

I think about all the labyrinths we walked together in
our latter years. You rushed through them, timing
yourself and crowing about your new record: *In
and out in seven minutes.* I circled around slowly,
knowing that I could trust the winding path to lead
me to my destination. I was a traveller without a map,
as P.K. Page put it in her essay "Traveller, Conjuror,
Journeyman," but I believed the labyrinth would
take me to where I needed to go. When I had breast
cancer, the labyrinth helped me accept the road
ahead, not knowing where it would lead. When
I thought about aging and approaching death, I
walked the labyrinth, feeling it would bring me
to greater understanding. But now that you aren't
with me, the path has disappeared and I am facing
dead ends, blind alleys. I see no way forward. My
labyrinth has become a maze.

It's one thing to be without a map if your path is
clear. But if you are directionless, the world around

you altered so vastly that you no longer know what your goal is, you're left in a state of confusion. Your death, Mike, leaves me disoriented, with no sense of direction, no clear destination.

I've always associated the word maze with a sense of magic. We used to speak of the similarity between the Maze and the Mage, the Magus. In fact, though, the etymology of maze relates not to magic but to the Old English verb *amasian*, which means to confound, to confuse, and is, of course, associated with the word amazement. Magicians speak of surprise as a key element in magic and in that, I think, lies a connection between the surprises of the maze and the potential for magic. So this is what I am hoping: when the labyrinth suddenly turns into a maze there is always the possibility of magic taking place.

If Ariadne is guide to the labyrinth, then P.K. Page is surely my guide to the maze:

I follow
the spiralling pathway over and over, run—
hoping to pass that place on the sharpening turn—
to grow small, then smaller, smaller still—and enter
the maze's vanishing point, a spark, extinguished.

I know what she means when she speaks of *the vanishing point* in the maze, the disappearance of self; of losing oneself not just in the sense of getting lost, but also in the sense of losing that part of the self which is ego, the self which attempts to control. In another poem, "Inebriate," Page says, *I had forgotten how to un-me myself.*

I've been feeling *un-me'd* and my labyrinth path is broken. But doesn't everything that has been broken offer new opportunities? As Leonard Cohen wrote in his song "Anthem," there is a crack in everything. *That's how the light gets in.* The maze is a place it can enter.

That's the paradox; what they now call disruptive innovation. The solution for a problem sometimes is only apparent when you span boundaries and see something beyond the obvious. I can move beyond what seems impossible, I tell myself. Becoming un-me'd and accepting what has been broken is part of finding my way.

During the last few years, we often spoke about death. Although you were generally, in your own words, insanely optimistic, you frequently expressed doubt about the future. *I don't think I will be sorry to leave this vale of tears,* you said, more than once. More and more, the everyday violence and depravity of the world depressed you. I found these lines in one of your notebooks:

Gallazin Locksmiths
Gang wars in Prince George
Teachers armed in Texas
Unlock the heart

And in the last months you kept grimly adding verses to your ongoing complaint about us being a part of the entitled, comfortable demographic:

We're all in the silver tsunami
We eat at the best spots in town
Those younger folk all must abhor us
They've no way of taking us down.

We're part of the silver tsunami
We dine where the dining is fine
All we need is fresh bread and salami
And gallons of on-the-house wine.

For us in the silver tsunami
Eating out is a frequent event
We spend so much money on lunches
Because we no longer pay rent.

I miss your quirkiness, your humour, your indestructible spirit in the face of everything. The way you saw things. My loneliness now is different from what it was in those early days when we were apart. Not the anxiety of *What if never?* but the certainty of *Never again.* Not the feeling of loneliness but the reality of being alone.

And yet, the reminders and the coincidences are often comforting. As I load up boxes of books in preparation for leaving our island home, I find messages everywhere. When I pack a pocket edition of Blake's *Songs of Experience* I discover a message from you on the inside cover:

> *So come kiss me,*
> *Now we're twenty*
> *Youth's a stuff will not endure,*
> *Money will though!*
> *And we've plenty*
> *Since our golden hearts are pure.*

> *Congratulations from your loving husband on your twentieth anniversary. And much, much love. M.*

In another book, I discover a weathered postcard of a Paris street scene on which you have written, *This card is old and frazzled mais tu! Es toujours jeune, toujours gai! Comme Paris! Bonne Fete, Bebé!* **Xox!**

Typing some of your old stories and papers and letters, transcribing from old typewritten papers on onion skin or yellowed photocopies, many with scratched out words and revisions in your familiar, large, swooping and rather clumsy script, I am flooded with love for you. It reminds me of something I read in an interview with Laurie Anderson after the death of Lou Reed, where she said, *I believe that the purpose of death is the release of love.* At first I considered this to be sentimental silliness and it made me angry. Now it makes sense. I experience this new surge of love, as in the courtship or the honeymoon. Wave after wave.

It truly is falling in love again, reading your letters and remembering those early days. To look objectively at the strange and wonderful way you had with words. I'm determined to keep you close, to cleave to you, across the enormous gulf. This, the final stage of our marriage, is full of meaning.

I sometimes think of our life in musical terms. Before I met you, it was a *Rondo Capriccioso*, quick but aimless. Our courtship could be called *Vivace*, lively and fast and full of life. There was no thought of grief or loss. Our long marriage unfolded in a comfortable, seemingly endless way as a lovely *Andante*. And then, mourning, endless sorrow, the *Doloroso* section. Finally, of course, there is the *Finale*, or the *Coda*, which can go on for a long time. The *Finale* brings disparate and paradoxical sections together in a way that reveals a life, a whole. Like the *Epilogue* of a novel, it ties up all loose ends.

I hum the five-note pattern that was once my singing exercise, *Me ma mah mo moo*, rising in semitones. *Do re mi re do.* Now I think of it as one, two, three, two, one, the description of where I am now in my life journey, alone again after being a twosome and a threesome. *Life journey!* you would sputter. What's this *journey* business? You thought the word was horribly overused in a dumbed down, new age way. *What isn't a journey these days? The journey of mental illness... the journey of post-secondary education... the journey of discovering Asian cuisine.*

I began alone and had been learning to deal with aloneness when you and I joined up as a twosome. We had great good time as a duo, and then we had Alison and we became that happy trio. When she grew up and left home, we had to learn how to become two again. At first I found it hard.

It's like learning how to ride a bicycle when you were used to a tricycle, a friend said, and that helped. Eventually, it became a very contented time. We reframed ourselves as a couple. You sang songs like, *Grow Old With Me, the Best is Yet to Come.* Now it is about learning to ride the unicycle.

How to carry on? The world feels unsettled, personally and globally. All I can do is to navigate through each day by making the best choices I can, one step at a time. And cleave to you, while being cleft apart.

Not a lot of time left. Perhaps I can do a little good in the world. *Spread a little cheerfulness around,* you would say. And so, I tug on my cleft ear, feeling your absence and cleaving to the sense of your presence. A friend, newly in a happy relationship after being widowed for over ten years, tells me that she feels closer now to her dead husband than ever before. *He is with me,* she says, *he is a part of me and always will be.* I, too, begin to feel that you are an integral part of who I am, though I am still too aware of your presence as you to contemplate ever having another partner.

At a debate on angelic art at the Fondazione Archivio Storico, a senior clergyman, Father Renzo Lavatori, a leading Catholic angelologist, said that angels do exist but they are not as much seen as their presence is felt. He said they were like sunlight that refracts on you through a crystal vase. *More like shards of light,* he said. That sounds like the light you used to call *rays of glory. Glory rays.*

I seek the sun each morning and try to think that your energy is a part of it. I actually believe this. My *gedankenexperiments* always fail and I know that we can never again have a real conversation, yet there is a consciousness I can pursue that makes me feel closer to you. Especially when there are glory rays.

Last night I dreamt that you and Victor and I were taking a road trip together. I told you I was sorry to have given away so many of our books and wouldn't have done so if everyone hadn't been sure you were dead. You said it was okay, you were just happy to be on this trip. Victor was racing around the property of our B&B and the owner was concerned, but you just grinned and said there was nothing to fear. I was worried when Victor started chasing the owner's miniature Dachshund, but you said not to worry, that Victor would just hold the dog gently. I looked down to the end of the garden and saw that Victor had the little dog's head in his mouth. *See how gentle he is?* you said, and I said, *Yes, but the little dog looks unsettled.* Somehow that made us both break out laughing and then I woke up, happy to have spent the night with you. Was the dream about the jaws of death? Dismaying, yet okay?

I talk to you all the time and there is some satisfaction in this, even if you don't answer back. And, although I'm not sure about heaven, I do know that the past is real and that coincidences can be remarkable. The other night I'd been talking aloud to you, wishing you were with me. *I want you to speak to me!* I said aloud, unbearably bereft. The next morning Fred Wah sent me a link to a recording of the UBC reading you had spoken at 50 years ago with Fred and Lionel Kearns. February 1, 1963. I was there! I listened to the tape and heard your clear and unmistakable voice reading familiar poems, poems I remembered! Playing the tape I recalled being at that hall, listening to the three men—poets were always men in those days—and feeling proud to be associated with you. The first poems you read were familiar. I have copies of them in the file folder you labeled POMES, but I'd forgotten the last poem and there wasn't a written copy of it anywhere. It was titled *Three Stanzas for Someone Who is Going Away,* and I remember how avidly I listened as you read it.

Opens... opens...
Who can give it thanks
or deal with it at all save howling for joy?

Give up the North. Give the North back to himself.
Give up the West, where no one cuts down the single hemlock
or the four pines that look to the sea.

I could never speak directly to you.
I have a cold talent for the other way.
I will never leave off speaking to you.

How did Fred know to send me this recording at the moment when I so needed to have you near? I sit in our island kitchen, looking out to the mainland mountains, weeping, as I hear your voice on that long ago tape, so real and so present. I take comfort in believing that you will never leave off speaking to me.

In our wedding ceremony, Rev. Gardiner spoke of us "coming together to form a single life." He said, we would "enter a wider realm of being" in which we could be more fully ourselves "by the devotion to the shared life of both." We believed this was true for us and that we were able to face the world, as he predicted, "strong with the strength of two, wise with the wisdom of two and brave with the courage of two."

Now, in my bereavement, I'm learning to become one again. Alone, aware of my separateness, and entering a new realm of being, I am beginning to feel not lessened but empowered by all that we've been together. I've never liked that "glass half full, glass half empty" expression, but I'm starting to feel, not sadness at what I've lost, but comfort and even joy in what I've had. I can use our mutual strength and courage and wisdom to become the best I can be as an individual.

And that means doing many things differently. Attempting merely to carry on with the routines and activities and interests we had in our mutual life has left me feeling wounded, diminished and incomplete. Now I'm trying to define myself newly as a lone person responsible for herself and her actions, strong with the strength our union gave me. I've learned to deal with car repairs, take responsibility for household upkeep, and open tight lids on pickle jars. In this epilogue of our marriage, I begin to understand our past in a meaningful way. Not as in Caitlin Thomas's memoir, *Leftover Life to Kill*, but as Lewis suggests: bereavement as a separate and distinct phase of our continuing marriage. One in which we are apart and yet together, cleft, yet cleaving to each other. In our Epilogue, I cleave to you, Mike. I talk to you.

Michaelangelo
Mio marito.
Mio angelo
I will never leave off speaking to you.

This shaking keeps me steady. I should know.
What falls away is always. And is near.
I wake to sleep, and take my waking slow.
I learn by going where I have to go.

The Waking, *Theodore Roethke*

Surviving

aster 2017. Another year has passed. More than a year, I have survived the day of our fiftieth wedding anniversary, an event for which we'd planned to have a celebration, never imagining that we wouldn't be together. I've survived the 5th anniversary of your death.

I'm surviving, which simply means that I have outlived you, but you have not disappeared from my life. Each night I envision the drift of stars, which is now your home, hoping you will appear to me in my dreams. Often you do. Each morning, I try to meet the day with your courage, your joy in life. My memories of our life together are part of who I now am and, despite the occasional jab of stark pain, there is solace in knowing that, in this way, you are with me. Or close. I keep reminding myself that *What falls away is always. And is near.*

I'm trying to cross over the dimensions of space and time in order to experience fully the bereavement phase of our marriage, our epilogue.

And it's more than surviving. Recently, while admiring an unusual cloudscape, the sun lighting up the sky after a storm with that peculiar greenish blue colour that appeared in some of your father's paintings, I felt a sudden surge of joy. It is a rare pleasure, that cyan shade, and you claimed it was your dead father colouring the heavens. Perhaps you are helping to do that work.

Things are changing for me, and I am gaining a new perspective. In literature, an epilogue can give a character a chance to speak from her own experience, to add new insights in her own voice, maybe even to change the focus of the story and its significance. It transports us to a distinct perspective and allows a broader view, one that crosses over and perhaps bridges. In there is the coda, from the Latin *cauda*, meaning *tail*. These concluding passages are supposed to "round out" a work.

It's time to round things out. Whether I like it or not, I'm still here, still alive, and life goes on. When I was writing my thesis on the literature of old age, my advisor, Dr. Constance Rooke, spoke to me about how in our lives we experienced all the functions of literature: the author, the protagonist, the editor, the reviewer. I like that metaphor. I like to think that I'm still at the editing stage, not yet at the life review, and that I can still make a few changes in my life story and work towards a good and meaningful ending. That doesn't mean forgetting our past, nor trying to replace it. Instead, it means finding new depths within myself and bringing them to the surface.

Years ago, a dear friend lost her only child to the recklessness of a drunk driver. For months afterward I often awoke in the middle of the night, trying to imagine how it would be possible for her to carry on. I remember jotting down these lines in a message to her:

Who will you be when you do not laugh?
Where will you go when there is no home?
Dig. Dig deep.
Find a new source. A new well.

After a long and painful struggle, my friend and her partner have made a new life for themselves. Each year they go to Cambodia to build homes for homeless people and to oversee the building of schools and the construction of wells. Their grief is endless but they have found a new source of purpose in their lives. Through the legacy of their daughter's tragic death, they have created a community, both locally and internationally, that works collaboratively to improve the lives of impoverished children.

Now I repeat my own words to myself—*Find a new source. A new well*—and I'm beginning to get some ideas about how to proceed.

Many of my bereaved friends, men especially, have remarried, often quite quickly, and they've picked up their old lives, the new partner slipping almost seamlessly into the place of the old. With their new partner they go on the same outings, attend the same dinner parties, enjoy the same holidays to the same old places as they've done in the past; it is as it was.

I see nothing wrong with this, but it will not be so for me. For one thing, of course, the opportunity may not arrive. I am not for all markets, as Rosalind said to Phoebe, and it is the case that old women do not usually have the options that men have. But the real reason is that I have no empty space to be filled. You are still with me, Mike, and I intend to live out our marriage, faithfully and fully, through this final phase.

It's a phase that requires a different kind of work. I don't want to become *woo woo*, but I believe there is spiritual work I can now do, work for which I never had time in our busy life together. I think of the Zen masters' advice: *Remember the face you had before you were born.* The original face, the true self, the soul.

For a long time, I've been depending on the wrong sort of spirit, too often turning to alcohol to improve my mood. I plan to cut back on the drinking, which together we frequently enjoyed to excess. Now the cheer that alcohol gives me is short-lived and I end up more depressed the next day. I'm learning that there is the true spirit, and there are also false spirits.

Lately, I have been thinking about your spirit. Through the years I became familiar with your body and your mind, but it is only now that I have a strong sense of your spirit.

I also want to do some useful work. There's much to be done in this damaged and dismantling world. I can't do anything on a large scale, but I'm doing some volunteer work where I live, helping non-profit organizations and serving on the board of the conservatory of music. I send cheques abroad to help people who have had so little of the comforts I've enjoyed. The good fortune that my family and I have had must be shared.

It's time to stop feeling sorry for myself and being critical of others. Instead it's time to practice kindness. As someone said, *Be kind, for everyone you meet is fighting a harder battle.* It could be true, even though it's hard not to feel that there's nothing worse than my own loss. But one has no way of knowing what grief others feel.

Grief is a permanent part of me. I will never "get over" your death. The British poet, playwright and physician Dannie Abse, in his memoir *The Presence*, notes that, months after his wife had died, a friend, seeing him in the company of a young woman, thoughtlessly said, "So you've got over it then," to which Abse replied vehemently, "I'll never get over it." So it is for me.

But I do find myself experiencing joy again. I am paying attention to the world around me—the sky, the sea, the people, the animals. *Rocks, and stones, and trees.* All of it. Even the insects. I like to think of the haiku by Issa: *Insects on a bough, floating downriver, still singing.*

As an old woman, I turn my thoughts to Minerva, the Roman goddess of wisdom. When Hegel wrote that Minerva's owl takes flight only with the twilight closing in, he spoke about philosophy painting its gray on gray and said "then has a form of life grown old, and with gray on gray it cannot be rejuvenated, but only known."

Writing this book has been like walking a labyrinth. It was necessary to go to the heart of things and then circle back, returning to how it all began and where it led. I realize that I cannot resurrect the past, but I can recall it. By exploring what was, by returning to the place where we started, I do, in Eliot's words, *know that place for the first time.* And the knowing brings satisfaction.

There are times when everything feels very close, when indeed what has fallen away feels very near. There was an extraordinary moment during my recent visit to Montreal, a trip that had been our annual pilgrimage. I was sitting in the kitchen with our nephew Ken as he was preparing dinner. I was rifling through a notebook that had once been yours. I told Ken how happy it made me to read these jottings. For example, I said, he writes,

Sorting out what's real. Music? Food when you're hungry feels very real.

We both laughed at the familiar sentiment.

And, listen to this one, I said, and read:

Brussels sprouts
sliced fine
pancetta in strips
salt
pepper
lemon juice
olive oil

No matter. I must have it!

Ken looked at me in astonishment. He was slicing Brussels sprouts at that very moment and exclaimed, "I gave him that recipe!" He pointed to the stove and continued, "There are strips of pancetta in the frying pan! I am making it for dinner."

Well, you said you must have it! It really felt as though you were with us and we were all happy. We drank a toast to you.

At the end of *A Grief Observed*, C.S. Lewis, struggling with the question of how to retain faith in a time of intense grief and loss, returns to an image of God as intelligence and love. For me, reflecting on what it is like to have lost you, I find myself overwhelmed with love for you and for what we had together.

And many things bring me pleasure. A few days ago, on reading that NASA had discovered a cluster of seven Earth-sized planets in a solar system about 40 light years away, each potentially capable of hosting liquid water and life, I felt sheer joy. It is a vast universe and there is much out there in the stardust that is beyond our understanding.

Here on earth there is also much to delight me. Increasingly aware that I am merely a miniscule speck of a creature on an impossibly tiny planet within that inconceivably infinite universe, I feel keen appreciation for the beauty of the living world and gratitude for the life I have here. Somewhere out in the endless stretches of time and space there may be echoes of our time here together but, in any case, inexplicably, I do not feel I am alone.

As I look out to the ocean, my mind drifts back to lazy summer afternoons, when we'd meet neighbours on the beach. I see clearly how the scene unfolds: the distance, the mainland mountains, a pale blue, lighter than the sky, deeper than the ocean and a slight wind rippling the waters, each wave glittering in the summer sunshine. I'm inching my way in to the water, just up to my ankles when I see you race across the shoreline and plunge into the ocean shouting, *"Cowabunga, boys and girls, Cowabunga!"* That was

Chief Thunderbird's greeting on *The Howdy Doody Show*, a fifties radio program that was a childhood favourite of yours. The Urban Dictionary says it originates from the word *How* morphing to *Cow* and that an *abunga* was just added for "silly kid— or those with Peter Pan syndrome—fun." That fits!

You swim quickly out and around the buoy, returning to the house just as I finally begin my swim. By the time the rest of us settle back on the rocks to dry off, you are back on the beach, fully dressed, grinning triumphantly, brandishing a silver tray that carries sparkling glasses of Prosecco.

These days, such memories strengthen me and bring me contentment. Through them I can believe you are everywhere, always, and with me in some form. That's how I am able to carry on.

Cowabunga, Mike. Cowabunga!

Acknowledgements

Members of my wonderful writing group supported me from the early days of my grief through to my writing and submission of this manuscript. Patricia Young and Dede Gaston were especially helpful with editorial suggestions. My friends Pauling Butling, Kathy Crandall, Ross Fraser, Judith Mackay, Liza Potvin and Jay Ruzesky read parts of the manuscript and offered useful suggestions. Gwyneth Evans read a late version of the entire manuscript with a sharp editorial eye and a helpful hand. Thanks to Rachel Wyatt for her friendship and for allowing me to quote the poem she attributes to my dog Victor and thanks to the Estate of PK Page for permitting me to quote her work. Thanks to Fred Wah for sending me the recording of the UBC reading.

I am greatly indebted to everyone at Oolichan Books—Randal MacNair, Carolyn Nikodym, and Ron and Patricia Smith—for their editorial support and suggestions. Working with Carolyn has been an especial pleasure. I am also grateful for Vanessa Croome's work in designing the cover and to Bill Pennell for the owl photograph.

I could not have written *Minerva's Owl* without the love and support of my daughter Alison, her husband Alex, my granddaughter Charlotte, and other family members and friends. As well, I have deep appreciation of the Hospice staff and volunteers for always being there.

Throughout the writing of this book, I was strengthened by recalling the days and years of my marriage to Mike and felt sustained by his spirit.

CAROL MATTHEWS has worked as a social worker, community worker, and Dean of Human Services and Community Education at Malaspina University-College (now Vancouver Island University) between 1988 and 1999. In 1999 she was awarded the Association of Community Colleges National Award for Excellence in Leadership. In addition to teaching and consulting activities, she has served as a director on a number of local and provincial boards and committees. In 2008 she was awarded an Honorary Doctorate of Letters Degree from Vancouver Island University (VIU). In 2012, was awarded the Order of B.C. in recognition of achievement and commitment to her local community, and In January of 2013, she was awarded the Queen Elizabeth II Diamond Jubilee Medal.

Her short stories have appeared in a number of literary publications, including *Grain Magazine*, *Prism*, *Room* and *The New Quarterly*, and she is the winner of the 2017 Jacob Zilber Prize for Short Fiction. She frequently publishes reviews in *Malahat* and *Event* and has also published articles in several educational journals. Articles published in the *Journal of Relational Child and Youth Care Practice* were collected and published as *The First*

Three Years of a Grandmother's Life (2006). A collection of short fiction, *Incidental Music* was published by Oolichan Books (2007). *Reflections on the C-Word: At the Centre of the Cancer Labyrinth*, a cancer memoir, was published by Hedgerow Press (2007). *Questions for Ariadne: The Labyrinth and the End of Times* was published by Outlaw Editions (2011). With Liza Potvin she has co-authored an epistolary account called *Dog Days* (2010) and she has also edited a collection of dog poetry called *Victor's Verses* (2002).

Other Books by Carol Matthews

Fiction

Incidental Music: Short Stories

Non-Fiction

The First Three Years of a Grandmother's Life

Reflections on the C-Word: At the Centre of the Cancer Labyrinth

Dog Days (co-authored with Liza Potvin)

Questions for Ariadne: The Labyrinth and the End of Times

My Faculties at Large by Mike Matthews, edited by Carol Matthews